D1084974

GERTRUDE STEIN

A BIOGRAPHY OF HER WORK

DONALD SUTHERLAND

Gertrude Stein

A BIOGRAPHY OF HER WORK

GREENWOOD PRESS, PUBLISHERS
WESTPORT, CONNECTICUT

TO MARCEL THOUVIOT DE CONINCK

CONTENTS

1. The Elements

This will be to explain as much as I understand of what Gertrude Stein did in writing.

To explain first how she began, by the leading ideas around her at the time. The work of William James and Hugo Münsterberg, with whom she studied at Radcliffe, can represent her intellectual surroundings in say 1895.

The central object of concern for James and Münsterberg and for many others at that time was the consciousness. Physiology, psychology, and metaphysics were all brought at once to bear on the consciousness as a problem. Was it a substantive entity, an epiphenomenon, a relation, a function, or what?

The consciousness had become problematical but so far it had not been displaced as the central object of concern by the subconscious or by behavior. Behavior was still a subject for ethics or the demonstration of something else.

And while the subconscious was being very much investigated it generally belonged to physiology, or brain facts, and not to mind facts, as they then made the distinction. The secondary and tertiary personalities of hysterical cases were considered conventionally as split-off parts of a total conscious personality, and rather sadly stupid. There was nothing seductive about them. The previous exaggerations of von Hartmann (1868) about the subconscious as a more gifted double of the conscious personality were standing objects

1

of ridicule, and as for what was to come, Freud and miscon-
structions of Freud did not yet count at Radcliffe. In 1894
James had published a notice of one of the first articles by
Freud and Breuer, on hysteria, but the *Traumdeutung* did
not appear until 1900 and the great doctor in person did not
burst upon New England until 1909. Before that, anything
like the surrealist trust in the subconscious was hardly likely.

Gertrude Stein like everyone else investigated the consciousness, and in 1896 she and a friend named Leon M.
Solomons published the results of some experiments they
had made in automatic reading and writing. The purpose of
the experiments was not to exploit a disreputable or at least
pathological subconscious but to show that motor automatism in the normal subject with his conscious attention volun-
tarily distracted was capable of the elementary feats performed by the second personalities in hysterical cases. This
in turn was to show that the "second personality" was an
unnecessary hypothesis for explaining hysterical phenomena.
Hysteria, by disordering the conscious attention, merely let
the basic automatism function freely. "We *would* not, the
histerique *can* not, attend to these sensations [of automatic
activity]. Whatever else hysteria may be then, this, at least,
seems most probable. It is a *disease* of the attention." [1]

This basic automatism was not yet thought of glowingly
as the normal subconscious, and even the notion of the
subliminal consciousness is treated rather briskly by Mr.
Solomons and Miss Stein in passing. Out of mock deference
to that theory they distinguish a "conscious consciousness."

The texts produced automatically are dealt with loftily and
humorously, and all connected thought in the texts is suspected of being an interruption by the conscious consciousness. "The stuff written was grammatical, and the words and

1. "Normal Motor Automatism," *Psychological Review*, III
(1896), No. 5, 511. By permission of the American Psychological
Association, Inc.

phrases fitted together all right, but there was not much connected thought. The unconsciousness was broken into every six or seven words by flashes of consciousness, *etc.* Here is a bit more poetical than intelligible.

" 'When he could not be the longest and thus to be, and thus to be, the strongest.' " [2]

This was, to the experimenters, curious enough but scarcely promising for literature. When the literary writing of Gertrude Stein came it was in full consciousness, written and to be read so. She said this and said it often but as her work did not look it she was normally not believed. The automatic passage [3] quoted above does look exactly like some of her later work. It is now not a question of belief so much as of understanding how her work was conscious and clear, objectively clear, and at the same time did not look it.

The reasons for this resemblance begin not in the question of the subconscious, whether hysterical or normal, but in the consciousness itself, as of 1895. Since the consciousness had become problematical its nature and procedures were examined very closely. It had replaced the soul and thus inherited what was left of religious and ethical concern, all the anxieties of personal identity. It was a serious matter to find the consciousness might be not only divisible but submersible. Janet's famous patient Lucie, who came in three layers, was the real Cleopatra of the late century, threatening

2. "Normal Motor Automatism," *loc. cit.*, p. 506.
3. In *Everybody's Autobiography* (Random House, 1937) Gertrude Stein says (p. 266) that Solomons did the reporting of these experiments, and she, being younger and docile, just agreed, though she did not really think the writing was automatic. "We always knew what we were doing." It is difficult to say anything about it now, but most likely the distraction of attention did help at least to destroy any awareness of complexes of reference beyond the words written, and allowed the words to be treated as objects and entities rather than as signs or symbols of something else. This may have been the beginning of a word sense that became dominant in her writing much later, in 1911.

3

the empire of right reason. It may seem no discovery now, but it was noticed that even the concentrated unified conscious consciousness as an observed fact or process does not move of itself in logical propositions which can be expressed in Aristotelian grammar or its extensions by subordinate clauses and ellipses and qualifications. The simple faith in reason or emotion as the base and meaning of writing, as with classicism and romanticism, was no longer possible.

The trouble was not at all confined to Radcliffe. Quite evidently the whole major literary movement of the early 20th century, with Proust, Joyce, Dorothy Richardson, Virginia Woolf, and the rest, was immensely occupied with this problem, both as a philosophical problem and as a problem of expression or form. This is common knowledge and known roughly as the stream of consciousness. James called it that but he also seems to have preferred calling it the stream of thought, which makes a difference, by including positive activity, choosing.

What will make not small but considerable differences among those novelists and Gertrude Stein is the differing conception of the contents or movements of consciousness, the conception of time or the sense of it, and the methods of forcing the words and composition to encompass or express the subject.

It makes a difference if the consciousness is thought of as in the main passively registering consecutive sensuous impressions and feelings. Out of that can be made the work of English ladies like Dorothy Richardson and Virginia Woolf, the intimate journal or a very rich and formal poetry after Keats. Again if the consciousness is taken as including at any moment a whole or partial past, as the person is his own biography, a Proust can make the most of it. If the consciousness is taken to imply at any moment a whole racial or mythological past, a Joyce can express it by sonorities of reference and verbal orchestration. And here it makes

4

a great difference whether the literary form is extended from the logical tradition to convert the illogical material to itself, as with Richardson, Woolf, and Proust, or whether the form is directed more or less completely by the qualities and behavior of the material, or rather by the terms of the experience of the material.

What then was the consciousness and how did it operate according to James and Münsterberg? And what did Gertrude Stein make of it, having a mind of her own?

Münsterberg remained true to the consciousness as an entity in the tradition of Kant and Wundt, but James suddenly in 1895 declared that it was not an entity but if anything a relation. This created a scandal, for James had himself maintained throughout his great book, *Principles of Psychology*, published in 1890, that the consciousness was an entity. His defection from the intellectualist position in 1895 was followed gradually by more and more agreement with Bergson, and finally by the invention of pragmatism and radical empiricism. Gertrude Stein was at Radcliffe during the first and worst of the agitation, before James had fully developed his new positions. It would be neat but absurd to say that she subscribed for life to any of his old or new formulations, especially since James himself was notorious for provoking his students to do their own thinking and for insisting that ultimately one's philosophical beliefs are determined by personal temperament. Also there is the pleasant story Gertrude Stein tells, how some years later when he saw her pictures by Matisse and Picasso, in Paris, he gasped and said he had always told her she should keep her mind open. While she was a favorite pupil she was not his creature. He did not have creatures.

Still she could scarcely have helped being deeply influenced by the new crisis in the question of consciousness and the way it was put. In the *Psychology* James had defined the consciousness as the passing thought, a momentary sec-

5

tion of the stream of consciousness. The passing thought was itself the thinker. It was in itself final and simple, regardless of the time, tendencies, purposes, origins, and complications of its objects. Considering what the soul had once been, this consciousness of 1890 was not much of an entity, pared to next to nothing with Occam's razor, to the bare minimum that would explain the given phenomena; but James concluded that even that much of a substantive was not needed and the "consciousness" was a relation or a function. The word was still used in the psychological laboratory under Münsterberg, but it was more precise to speak of "attention," as being verifiable in the laboratory, and James had already said before 1890 that consciousness was equivalent to attention, or vice versa.

But for creative purposes the difference was that instead of the substantives, thought and thinker, there was now the gerund or participle: thinking. Gertrude Stein was by nature passionately given to the intellect, but all was not lost in losing the final reality of the thought and thinker. As a tough and healthy mind she could be just as ferociously excited if not more so by thinking. After all, the ways of thinking were as real as the forms of thought. The vital consequence of this new position for literature was that the consciousness was no longer a receptacle with one or many contemplated things with their qualities sitting in it at a time; the consciousness was now an activity going on. Relations were more important to it, more essential, now, than substantives. Already in his *Psychology* James had made the distinction between substantive thoughts and transitional thoughts, and declared it should be recognized that we have a definite feeling of "if" and of "and" and of "but" and of "whether," and Gertrude Stein later gave such words all their importance, but they get all their importance from the conception of consciousness as thinking in relation.

Whether or not the idea became perfectly disengaged at

6

Radcliffe at that time in the thick of the crisis, the idea that present thinking is the final reality was to be the axis or pole of Gertrude Stein's universe, and her work from the beginning was oriented and reoriented upon that idea.

Such a persuasion is neither validated nor invalidated by what happens to fashions in philosophy or psychology. If structuralism gives way to functionalism and functionalism gives way to behaviorism and so on, it curiously makes no difference. As with the theory of humors to the Elizabethans, any philosophical or scientific theory is to an artist a working articulation of the universe, a language or an alphabet, with which to express experience. Everything depends on the eloquence, completeness, and exactitude with which the living experience is expressed by the language used. Oddly enough when theories perish as truth or as accomplishments, they often survive as a language in the arts. The only important thing for literature is whether the theory used as a language is going to look in the future like a dialect or like a diction.

At all events, the terms and objects of present thinking in average passive attention—receptivity—are, manifestly, colored by memory and anticipation and elaborate preconception, all of which makes for a general diffusion and dimness. Art can either clarify this penumbra or periphery—as Proust did—or suppress it. It is true that art can also exploit it, but such an art is journalism or one of romantic suggestion or belongs to a closed culture where the suggestions can be complete and definite.

The means of suppression or suspension are mainly a sharpening of the focus on the present, the disconnection of the object from causality and purpose. For all the Teutonic enthusiasm of his little book, *Principles of Art Education*, Münsterberg makes this function of art fairly clear. While uttering the general proposition that science is connection and art is isolation, he exhorts the public as follows: ". . . let

7

us only once give our whole attention to that one courageous, breezy wave, which thunders there against the rock; let us forget what there was and what there will be; let us live through one pulsebeat of experience in listening merely to that wave alone, seeing its foam alone, tasting its breeze alone,—and in that one thrill we have grasped the thing itself as it really is in its fullest truth." [4]

Gertrude Stein gradually succeeded in disengaging not only substantives like waves but the relations of thinking from their scientific and pragmatical penumbra and did, later, in *The Making of Americans*, reach her element, the continuous present.

It is an interesting if idle question how it happened that she took this rather disconnected and disembodied passing thought or present thinking as hers. No doubt part of it was the intense interiority of her adolescence from which she had barely emerged on coming to Radcliffe, and part of it surely was her Jewish gift of extreme attention to abstractions. That she was personally disconnected from any native or local context is again partly a Jewish situation and partly the accident of being born in Pennsylvania, traveling in France and Austria, and living in California and Baltimore, all before turning up for college work at Radcliffe, in the deliquescence of New England and the Puritan tradition. This multiplied delocalization was not yet, I believe, the average American personal situation.

Another circumstance that could easily have inclined her to feeling the reality of such an orientation upon the exclusive present was her habit at Radcliffe of going to the opera, in the afternoon and at night. The opera as a form tends to be complete at every instant, it is in constant present activity, and it is of little or no interest what the reasons for it all are or how it will all come out. In any event Gertrude Stein kept

4. *Principles of Art Education* (Prang Educational Company, 1904), p. 23.

8

an affection for the opera as a form and wrote a good many operas or librettos later on. She said that music was for adolescents and this could easily have been true of the music of her adolescence as performed in Boston and in late Wagner, but at least the principle of the continuous present was more or less already there in the opera form. In actual opera it was rather the prolonged present, and indeed the prolonged present was the time of her first literary work, *Three Lives*. I will get around to that in the next chapter.

With the literary production of the time she had almost no direct connection. Swinburne and Meredith were endlessly rarefying and elaborating any casual theme and Pater had invented the hard gemlike flame, but none of it was anything radically to start from. It is very strange that when she could have started so well from Henry James she did not. Henry James had already made of his work a time continuum less of external events or things than of intellect in constant activity upon their meaning. He recognized Proust as having done very much the sort of thing that he himself was trying to do, but there is a difference. Where Proust expands by more and more particular context and elaborating more and more tenuous relationships within a universe of concrete and sensuous experience, James tended to schematize the exterior and the sensuous to mere melodrama, a mere frame or boogiewoogie bass for the real rich drama which was for him that of ethical dubiety, the considerations of terribly conscious persons.

This disembodiedness, this discontextuated activity is by no means a peculiarity of Henry James and Gertrude Stein. Its beginning may well be colonial Puritanism, in which there is little enough interest and no excitement but the interior struggle of the soul with sin. Transcendentalism and Hawthorne, Melville, Thoreau, Emerson, and even Henry Adams are all variously part of the same thing; but the pragmatic and effective suppression of the objective context, the dis-

9

engagement of a single simple theme or motion, is more immediately illustrated at the end of the 19th century in America by the complete development of endless straight railroads with trestles and tunnels, by the beginning of the skyscraper, the automobile and the airplane. This peculiar American pleasure in continuous, even, present movement in less and less context did not on the whole extend to literature, not for the general public who enjoyed automobiles, western movies, airplanes, and endless aimless travel very much.

If this disengaged present thinking had these approximations in the past and these parallels in the physical world, thus coming rather naturally, how was it related to the whole person doing it, to time, to its objects and terms both interior and exterior, and so forth?

There was naturally the animal or living creature doing the thinking, and the vitality of thinking was continuous with the vitality of the person. That is to say the thinking was alive, not in a religious but in a biological way. William James talks of pulses of consciousness as Münsterberg does of pulse beats of experience. Gertrude Stein in her independent experiments on attention and fatigue in Harvard and Radcliffe students concluded that habits of attention are reflexes of the complete character of the individual. The phrase "habits of attention" is clinical for "ways of thinking."

While thinking is alive as a function of the whole creature, the whole creature is not an activity but a substantive structure. It is thought of as a complete present fact, biologically or medically, and so perfectly classifiable as a type. It is called a character, not with ethical connotations particularly, but as a shape or consistency, as definite as the ossature of a fish or a horse. Gertrude Stein made charts of the human types she described in *The Making of Americans*. If people change it is very little if at all within their lives, but by the generation or the century. Within the single individual the diffusion

10

or concentration, the gentleness or toughness, the ways of attack or defense or dependency, of desire or strength or cowardice, do not essentially vary. In short the whole composition of the character can really be present in any moment, in the continuous present, and not as a thing remembered, not as an accumulation of personal history.

If the character does not change, if its interior and exterior
nd if it is
ter and the
writer, the
without a
evant acci-
stantly new
g, an exist-
ctually that
ntly assert-
nent to mo-
Making of

aracters are
s, a sort of
a but as individuals. Proust comes partly out of Bergson and impressionism, partly out of Chateaubriand and de Nerval, and ultimately out of the late classical tradition of Ovid and Apuleius. It is really extraordinary that the exotic Proustian character, "a giant in Time," saturated with incident and surrounded by depths of meaning and association, should have been perfectly convincing to educated Americans, and that *The Making of Americans,* written so rigorously on our own principles, should seem exotic and outrageous. But the educated American would still rather visit the Cloisters than the Pentagon building, which after all is to us as the Escorial is to the Spanish or Versailles to the French.

The full demonstration of the persistence, not the develop-

11

ment, of the whole living personality through time came with *The Making of Americans* and the early portraits, but the project is already very much begun in *Three Lives*. She began writing *Three Lives* while translating the *Trois Contes* of Flaubert and while constantly looking at a portrait of a woman by Cézanne. The implications here are nearly inexhaustible, but for the moment it can be said that the difference between Gertrude Stein and Proust is the difference between Cézanne and the impressionists. The complexities of accident, light, and circumstance are reduced to a simple geometrical structure, a final existence addressed to the mind. It is tempting to take this situation also as accounting for Proust's dislike of Flaubert who in the previous century had reduced Chateaubriand to a steady present reality, but that is not my subject. Still, there is a phrase in Gertrude Stein's portrait of Cézanne, that he was "settled to stay," [5] which expresses where she and Cézanne and Flaubert were in time, and what Proust and the impressionists and Chateaubriand were not. They were something else, with the loveliness and elegance and brilliance of being provisory, of transience, but very different.

If thinking is alive and final and continuous with the whole creature, what are its basic ways of doing? Gertrude Stein said she always had an impulse for elemental abstraction, and the primary terms of present thinking are the foundation of all her work. Whether they are to be taken as ideal existences or as procedures of thinking or as objects of thinking, they are absolutely valid so far as any human thinking goes. If Plato makes the Same and the Other objective elements in the universe, and if James talks about the feeling of sameness and the feeling of difference as events in the mind, identity and difference are for human purposes final. Relations like *if* and *and, in* and *out, up* and *down, left*

5. *Portraits and Prayers* (Random House, 1934), p. 11.

and *right*, and so forth are final intellectual constructions. It is to them and the like that all sensations and complexities must be referred for meaning to the mind. They may involve emotion, in the sense of muscular disposition, but that is another question. They belong to the mind, as music belongs to the ear before it belongs to the possibly dancing body.

This looks perfectly natural and simple but its meaning for literary composition is a little more complicated. Most literature does not address itself directly to the final terms of present thinking but to the vague memory of complex unresolved situations and the provisory attitudes taken toward them. In short, most literature is based on sympathetic reminiscent emotion, or if you like upon anxiety, and not upon completely present disengaged thinking. This makes a difference for example between classicism and romanticism, between Mozart and Wagner, and a difference between what Gertrude Stein later called human nature and the human mind.

In her *Autobiography of Alice B. Toklas* she made this explanation:

Gertrude Stein, in her work, has always been possessed by the intellectual passion for exactitude in the description of inner and outer reality. She has produced a simplification by this concentration, and as a result the destruction of associational emotion in poetry and prose. Nor should emotion itself be the cause of poetry and prose. They should consist of an exact reproduction of either an outer or an inner reality.

It was this conception of exactitude that made the close understanding between Gertrude Stein and Juan Gris.

Juan Gris also conceived exactitude but in him exactitude had a mystical basis. As a mystic it was necessary for him to be exact. In Gertrude Stein the necessity was intellectual, a

13

pure passion for exactitude. It is because of this that her work has often been compared to that of mathematicians and by a certain french critic to the work of Bach.

Picasso by nature the most endowed had less clarity of intellectual purpose. He was in his creative activity dominated by spanish ritual, later by negro ritual expressed in negro sculpture (which has an arab basis the basis also of spanish ritual) and later by russian ritual. His creative activity being tremendously dominant, he made these great rituals over into his own image.[6]

While the precise geometries of Gris correspond to the very close manipulations of elemental abstractions that make even the earliest of her writing, it is very important to know that these elemental abstractions did not have for her a mystical or ritualistic meaning or a tragic meaning. Her art like that of Henry James or that of Mozart was a thoroughly intellectual and secular art, essentially, and in the great sense, comic.

Her attention was in a way trained to the comic and to secular finesse from the beginning, to an exclusive occupation with extremely fine likenesses and differences. The Harvard Psychological Laboratory under Münsterberg was an intellectual circus, and she was a highly trained performer. She engaged in experiments on such things as "Fluctuations of the Attention" and "The Saturation of Colors." In this last experiment, reported by Solomons, he says: ". . . to compare the mixtures of a very different intensity with regard to their saturation, with any degree of accuracy, seems at first a hopeless task. But with a little practice, beginning with large differences and working down, the judgement becomes quite possible, and eventually exceedingly accurate. Owing

6. *The Autobiography of Alice B. Toklas,* in *Selected Writings of Gertrude Stein* (Random House, 1946), pp. 174–175.

to the training required the experiments were made only by Miss Stein and the writer." [7]

There is an amusing kind of cubist circus in another experiment, conducted by W. G. Smith, on "The Place of Repetition in Memory," and with among other subjects one called *St.*:

Series of syllables were printed on slips of paper by means of a typewriter in such a form that the subject could easily read what was printed. In each series there were ten syllables forming one line; in each syllable there were three letters, the vowel being in the middle. Syllables which were too harsh in sound, or which might suggest too easily an intelligible word or phrase were rejected. No two successive syllables were allowed to have the same vowel, and the same consonant could recur only after several others had intervened. . . .

In the actual experiments the slip of paper bearing the syllables was inserted in a frame which was fastened behind an oblong horizontal opening in a screen made of black cardboard. Behind this opening and before the slip of paper was a shutter which could be raised or lowered at any moment. The subject, who sat at his ease before the screen, was required to read the series aloud, one syllable after another, at a rate determined by a metronome standing near him, etc. The object of introducing the metronome was to assure that the subject should, as far as possible, give the same time and attention to each syllable. Where a series had to be repeated several times the subject made a pause of two beats each time he came to the end, and then began the repetition again. The shutter covering the series was raised only after the subject had given a signal that he was ready and had accommodated himself to the rhythm. [8]

7. *Psychological Review*, III (1896), No. 1, 51.
8. *Ibid.*, pp. 22–23.

The subject *St.*, in reproducing the series from *memory*, had a very high score of misplaced and incomplete syllables. But this extremely close attention to the smallest and most final elements of language or anything became constant in her thinking and in her work. From the beginning these elements were not simply perceived and judged or discriminated but formed part of an activity requiring extraordinary readiness and dexterity. A pretty example of this is an account by James, in this chapter on attention, of an early experiment by Münsterberg.

In a series of experiments the five fingers were used to react with, and the reacter had to use a different finger according as the signal was of one sort or another. Thus when a word in the nominative case was called out he used the thumb, for the dative he used another finger; similarly adjectives, substantives, pronouns, numerals, etc., or, again, towns, rivers, beasts, plants, elements; or poets, musicians, philosophers, etc., were co-ordinated each with its finger, so that when a word belonging to either of these classes was mentioned, a particular finger and no other had to perform the reaction. In a second series of experiments the reaction consisted in the utterance of a word in answer to a question, such as "name an edible fish," etc.; or "name the first drama of Schiller," etc.; or "which is greater, Hume or Kant?" etc.; or (first naming apples and cherries, and several other fruits) "which do you prefer, apples or cherries?" etc.; or "which is Goethe's finest drama?" etc.; or "which letter comes the later in the alphabet, the letter L or the first letter of the most beautiful tree?" etc.; or "which is less, 15 or 20 minus 8?" etc. etc. etc.[9]

Compare with this what Sherwood Anderson said of Gertrude Stein many years later:

9. *Principles of Psychology* (Henry Holt, 1890), I, 432–433.
16

She is laying word against word, relating sound to sound, feeling for the taste, the smell, the rhythm of the individual word . . . One works with words and one would like words that have a taste on the lips, that have a perfume to the nostrils, rattling words one can throw into a box and shake, making a sharp, jingling sound, words that, when seen on the printed page, have a distinct arresting effect upon the eye, words that when they jump out from under the pen one may feel with the fingers as one might caress the cheeks of his beloved. And what I think is that these books of Gertrude Stein do in a very real sense recreate life in words.[10]

It is true that words as manipulated by Gertrude Stein have a greater sensuous vividness and singly an independent life, but except for a very few lapses she never forgot that the word is an intellectual construction with an intellectual meaning, regardless of its sensuous qualities. Her manipulations almost invariably carry not only the body of the word but primarily its meaning.

The formal problem as usual coincides with the psychological or philosophical problem. If the substantive entity grows weak and fails to dominate its action and objects and relationships, the problem is also one of grammar. The Aristotelian sentence, with subject and predicate and their subordinates, either has to be extended or it falls apart or it has to be rescued.[11] James in the *Psychology* pointed out that the

10. Quoted by Carl Van Vechten in his introduction to *Selected Writings of Gertrude Stein*, p. xi.
11. In 1921 Gertrude Stein wrote, in *Operas and Plays* (Plain Edition, 1932), p. 124, "I do hate sentences." But a few years later, requiring a completely disembodied movement and organization for her writing, she rediscovered the relations and gestures of grammar as a sufficient expressive means, a sort of intellectual plastic or draughtsmanship in itself. The works combined in *How to Write* (Plain Edition, 1931) are protracted studies of the possibilities. Among them is a lovely and instructive piece called "Saving the Sentence," written in 1929.

sentence "Columbus discovered America in 1492," while it may be taken to be about Columbus or about America, is not a substantive object of thought except when written or conceived as Columbus-discovered-America-in-1492. "Nothing but this can possibly name its delicate idiosyncrasy. And if we wish to *feel* that idiosyncrasy we must reproduce the thought as it was uttered, with every word fringed and the whole sentence bathed in that original halo of obscure relations, which, like an horizon, then spread about its meaning." [12]

An intellectual passion for exactitude and clarity has no patience with fringes and delicate idiosyncrasies and horizons. Gertrude Stein would have written the sentence perhaps as sentences: Columbus. Discovered. America. In. 1492. Her literary problem was in the main one of recomposing such elements while retaining their original completeness and clarity. Repetition was of course a natural device for making something more of such elements, but I will describe her formal solutions later in writing about her works in order. For the moment the point is that the words and the elements of thought had become disengaged from their conventional groupings and relationships. It is no accident at all that new groupings should be acrobatic or like a circus, and that the actual circus was to dominate artistic fashions in Paris before long. Whether it passed into the Russian ballet or into the rather sentimental tragedy of Picasso's harlequins and clowns, the circus was in a way the paradigm for the art forms of that time. Gertrude Stein ran her circus with the merciless efficiency and reckless innocence of a Barnum or an Aristophanes. There was very little if any *vesti la giubba* about it.

They [Picasso and Gertrude Stein] talk about everything, about pictures, about dogs, about death, about unhappiness. Because Picasso is a spaniard and life is tragic and bitter and

12. *Principles of Psychology,* I, 275–276.

unhappy. Gertrude Stein often comes down to me and says,
Pablo has been persuading me that I am as unhappy as he is.
He insists that I am and with as much cause. But are you, I
ask. Well I don't think I look it, do I, and she laughs. He says,
she says, that I don't look it because I have more courage,
but I don't think I am, she says, no I don't think I am.[13]

Now, before examining the works directly, there are a few
general matters that can be settled. Why does for example
the automatic sentence "When he could not be the longest
and thus to be, and thus to be, the strongest" look so exactly
like some later Stein? For example:

Saints and their singing.
Saints and singing do not come to this as an ending. Saints
and singing. Read me by repetition. Saints and singing and a
mission and an addition.
Saints and singing and the petition. The petition for a
repetition.
Saints and singing and their singing.
Saints and singing and winning and.
Do not repeat yourself.[14]

Because the thought is not "connected" with any particular
context external to what is being said, because it proceeds
as an activity in time instead of heaping festoons of qualifica-
tion upon the subject, because it repeats and rhymes, making
an insistence and prolongation within the present thinking
to sustain it to realization, like a trilled note in music. Gertrude Stein once said the difference between her writing and
that of the insane was that you could go on reading hers. An
automatic bird cry may be very lovely but it does not hold
the attention like a musical composition. In short, whether

13. *The Autobiography of Alice B. Toklas,* p. 64.
14. *Operas and Plays,* p. 87.

Gertrude Stein used for her later work the stylistic suggestions already present in these automatic texts or not, the later work is a deliberate and perfectly conscious creation, given that consciousness was proceeding in an untraditional manner [15] and in disconnection from the practical context of events, values, and accidents, as conventionally interpreted.

The early works of Gertrude Stein, *Three Lives* and *The Making of Americans*, though the vocabulary and composition are unusual, do make a perfectly average comprehensible sense. For many critics these are her great and essential works. But the principle objections to them, that they are cold or dead or clumsy or inhuman, are impressions which unhappily kept her from being read seriously by any but a small fraction of the American public. The demands of the educated American public were for precisely the things her work was meant to destroy, biographical or historical emotion, vaguenesses of feeling and slurred ideas, all essential to the average educated American literary taste. They could get more of what they wanted from D. H. Lawrence—and from Proust, by ignoring his wit and his Rabelaisian side: that his "giants in Time" are true descendants of Gargantua. Even Joyce, with the stunted giants of *Ulysses*, was more to that taste. It was only when his giants reached their proper growth, in *Finnegans Wake*, that a coolness set in. With so little in Gertrude Stein's work to appeal to the biographical sense, the familiar personal emotions, it is no wonder her work looked dead or inhuman. The excitement of it was mental, but the intellect was, popularly and to the educated, dead. To Henry James and to Gertrude Stein the consciousness was very much alive, more brilliantly alive than human nature with all its biographies. Her work looked not only

15. There is a long if secondary tradition of non-Aristotelian procedure, including a good many Greeks, the Old Testament, and more recently Sterne.

20

academic but hairsplitting. Her terribly fine and close attention was applied to things of after all the first importance, although they were not yet important to the public at large. But just as the analyses of James and Proust which once seemed so infinitely delicate now appear broad and burly enough, and as the distinctions of color, line, and texture in Picasso are now obvious to any interior decorator or engineer, it may not be long before the methods of Gertrude Stein are generally taken to be, not Byzantine as Byzantine is normally understood, but as immediate and exciting as anything America has produced in this century.

2. THREE LIVES *and* THE MAKING OF AMERICANS

To make roughly an anatomy of *Three Lives*, from the broadest elements down, and beginning with narrative structure. Not only does *Three Lives* make a profitable exercise in literary anatomy but it contains already many principles which will stay for the later work of Gertrude Stein.

Simple narrative structure is when events are shown as leading from one to the other in temporal and causal succession until some conclusion such as death, marriage, riches, success, failure, or just arriving or going away is reached. The comparison of narrative structure to architecture is right, insofar as both a story and a building make an arrangement or an enclosed place for living, a field of presence for the mind, by which everything outside of it can be dismissed from concern. It functions like the frame of a picture, to isolate what goes on inside it for complete attention and realization. Or it can be like the flat surface of a picture, to which everything presented is referred for realization. Of course the plane of action in writing like the plane of flat space in painting is treated differently, multiplied or broken or scattered or tilted or even destroyed by certain writers in certain historical periods.

But history aside, why is it that anyone likes and accepts a simple consecutive story as the plane of reference for presenting life to the mind? Regardless of interest and suspense and conflict and surprise and so on, and quite regardless of folk tales and fairy tales being genito-urinary metaphors or something, why is it all so often done in narrative? One reason is that events following each other continuously and coming to a conclusion flatter or confirm our sense of causing and controlling and possessing what we do and of being really the object of what happens to us. No matter how awful what happens is, in a story it happens to somebody and somebody makes it happen and these agents and sufferers get a very concrete and solid meaning from the events, which we may not feel continuously that we have in our lives. Another reason could be that most of our physical activities, eating, walking, working, and making love, do go on in a continuous series of movements until a conclusion of some sort is reached. So narrative may be an objectification and so a stabilizing and a reassurance of this natural way of doing anything.

But if narrative is natural and likable and it is, why is it often so difficult and sometimes a falsification to use it? Just as the Doric temple could not contain the Roman or Romanesque or Gothic or Renaissance religious life, so a simple narrative structure often cannot contain the life, whether religious or secular. It is a nice game to match architectural and narrative styles, as Marivaux with the Trianon, or Proust with Palladio and the reflections and reverberations of the Venetian palaces which make a use of classicism, or even Gertrude Stein with Louis Sullivan, who established the theory as well as the fact of the skyscraper; but I wish to account for *Three Lives* historically awhile, more than to describe it by comparisons.

Happily the situation in narrative to Gertrude Stein when she began can be shown by "Un Coeur Simple," the story by Flaubert which she was translating when she began writing *Three Lives*, in particular the first of the stories "The Good Anna."

Flaubert if one likes was a naturalist, which means that his art was a mortification or resolution or reduction of romanticism, which in turn has a very clear relation to simple narrative, so we may begin there. If classicism is integrated by the equivalence of the inner life to the outer event, or by the feeling that they both exist in a closely interdependent relevance, romanticism can be taken to be the collapse of that unity. In romanticism the inner life proceeds in incoherence or syncopation with outer events. From their state of incoherence with present events, the romantics do look away to the past or future or just to foreign civilizations where the classical equivalence was or is or might be. The romantic is not an adventurer but an exile and a wanderer. Complete immediate narrative cannot be written because the main reality is away and what exists in the present is purely emotion and reflection or dreaming. Romanticism produces no architecture, not even revivals, but it does use the ruins of other styles to dream in. When the romantics write narrative it has to go on elsewhere, that is, to be real it has to be separate and exotic. Chateaubriand cannot write his autobiography without supposing himself already dead.

Flaubert intermittently came out of romanticism. The change was in ceasing to look away at a distant coherence and in looking at a present incoherence steadily. Flaubert naturally had no illusions about his bourgeois present, and it was perhaps more terrible to him than anything the romantics had to put up with, because he kept his attention more and more obsessively fixed upon it, but it was reality, the reality. And it was incoherent, or split. Flaubert, in *Madame Bovary*, synchronized or made contrapuntal, so to speak, the two separate parts of present reality, much as Cervantes had done it in *Don Quijote*. Just as the chivalric world of Don Quijote is as present and real as that of Sancho

24

Panza, so the romantic world of Emma Bovary is as real as that of Homais. It is their incoherent coexistence in the present which makes the whole orientation or thesis for the work of art. In "Un Coeur Simple," the dying Félicité, who is a simpler or nutshell Bovary, identifies her beloved stuffed parrot with the dove of the Holy Ghost, and this confrontation is a variant of the windmill which is a giant to Don Quijote. It is. grotesque, but precisely the grotesque is for these writers the first quality of the full reality. As early as 1838 Flaubert had invented a separate god of the grotesque, Yuk, and declared him to be as universal as death. The standard form for the representation of the final grotesque is tragicomedy, and the manner is irony, whether grim or gentle or desperate or resigned or whatever. It is within this range that "Un Coeur Simple" and then *Three Lives* were written.

Before going into the consequences of this orientation to form, one may here ask the question: Why Flaubert? Why his reputation in America? At the least his reputation has been for using *le mot juste* and having the perfect style. We used to like formal exactitude and perfection as we used to like it in motors. We also used to think that the actual was our business and realism of some sort our native method. Even our most elaborate myths started at Nantucket and Brooklyn Bridge. This prejudice no doubt had its influence on Gertrude Stein, but more immediately her studies under William James who was going to invent pragmatism, and her anatomical studies at Johns Hopkins, would have inclined her to the exhaustive precisions of Flaubert. And it was not Zola. There was no room in Zola for anything like the pragmatist proposition that truth is what you make it. Truth for Zola was simply and finally scientific causality, whether biological or social. For all his enormous energy, his moral courage, his easy way with solids and masses, he was intellectually gross. He was not a philosopher or a psychologist nor as a scientist more than an enthusiast. All of which may be nothing against his art, but it would very much keep him from influencing a young woman of Gertrude Stein's training, while the generally more professional mind and sensibility of Flaubert—within realism or naturalism—would attract her. She says in *Paris France* that she was very early interested in Zola as a realist but more interested in the Russian realists,[1] no doubt because the Russians eminently were dramatists of the incommensurability between the inner and the outer life.

At any rate, the difficulties of simple narrative structure under the strain of ambivalence or two bearings are well enough shown by the trouble between the main story and the interpolated stories of *Don Quijote*. The major theme, Quijote-Sancho, can never be brought to the certain progress and simple outlines of the interpolated romances. The irrelevance of the external events to the inner life they contain is exploited by Flaubert in the account of the route of the fiacre containing Emma and her lover, or the medical details of her death, or in the wanderings of Félicité about Le Havre. His famous technique of "dissociation"—as with the interweaving of the public speech with the conversation of Emma and Rodolphe—is exactly and obviously this thing. The technique, instead of "dissociation," is really the association of incompatibles.

The plan for presenting this dual or incoherent reality becomes naturally a simple series of confrontations of a person taken as the vehicle of the inner life, with people or situations representing the outer events. The confrontations or episodes can be more or less resolved or simply abandoned one by one, but the sequence of events has no meaning in itself except as an accumulation of demonstrations. Thus there is only an episodic structure concluded by the death of

1. *Paris France* (B. T. Batsford, 1940), p. 7.

the subject—Don Quijote, Emma Bovary, Félicité, the Good Anna.

An episodic structure was made disreputable as early as Aristotle, who was all for unity of external action, and the inner life except as ethics did not concern him. But if unity in terms of external events no longer accounts adequately for the full reality, what sort of unity or completion can there be? There are many answers to that, but one answer was the life of one person. Biography had already found that an adequate unity often enough, and the biographical convention had been useful in the novel since Marivaux and Richardson at least, but the life told about had had meaning as adventure, as an example of some virtue or vice, or simply as a figure as real and elaborate as a living person known for a long time. In the scientific climate of the 19th century the single life took on the meaning of a case history, or the natural and inevitable performance of any instance of a species. If man is the species the interest is less in the rare cases and sports than in the average and ordinary. The literary record of an ordinary life is not a documentation of the single case for its own sake or for the sake of adding to our knowledge of single cases, but a demonstration of how the single case expresses the essentials of the whole species or subspecies. To the naturalists the species man was above all the maladjusted animal, or, to avoid misunderstanding perhaps, the unadjustable animal. The subtitle of *Madame Bovary* is *Moeurs de Province*, or *Provincial Behavior*, and this does not mean that it is a documentation of the French provinces—which had come, mixed with other intentions, with Balzac, and was to come again with the vulgarization by Zola—but that it is a demonstration by a specific instance of the characteristic provincialism of the species man. Not being God, he is always in some province or other, whether he is restless or contented in it. The view is fatalistic and can be ironical. The epigraph to *Three*

27

Lives is the flat observation of Jules Laforgue,[2] "Donc je suis un malheureux et ce n'est ni ma faute ni celle de la vie." And when that has been settled, the intelligence is free from guilt and grievance, to go on and describe the behavior of the species. This really does not need any justification, but in these days of responsibilities and imperatives it is just as well to say that Homer and Shakespeare and Cervantes wrote from that same attitude, and that while a social purpose and reform and revolution do very well in their way, the virtue of art consists in seeing farther than that and more than that, whether the prospect glows or darkens.

It so happens, however, that the naturalists, with *Three Lives* in their wake, had among their significances an obvious social one. Flaubert was ferociously political, with a particular hatred for the middle class. His complaint against them was in the main their abject fear of being alive and the ineffable clumsiness of their behavior. His values were aristocratic. Gertrude Stein could naturally not take up a French political attitude. The American middle class if one can distinguish such a thing still had its health, and the remains of what might be called the New England aristocracy had nothing promising for the national life, either in the way of values or of impulse. She had settled the New England type rather brutally in her classifications at Radcliffe. And so soon after the Civil War the southern aristocracy could not be taken seriously. At all events the early work of Gertrude Stein accepts and loves the middle class as being the vital class in America. Very much later she had wicked things to say about our lower middle class,[3] but as late as *The Making of Americans* she said passionately, against other claims, that anything worth while had always come from the

2. Her bow to Laforgue, though it covers his fatalism, evidently cannot indicate any sympathy with his liking for von Hartmann's philosophy of the unconscious.

3. See *Wars I Have Seen* (Random House, 1945), p. 27.

middle class. Even if that is not entirely so, the attitude is far from foolish.

In *Three Lives* she deals with the poor, whom she had known as servants and patients in Baltimore, but there is very little if any political meaning to it. They are primarily human and not social types. She had what was then not a sentimental or programmatic but a natural democratic feeling that any human being was important just as that, as a human being. This feeling was no doubt reinforced and made confident by her philosophical and medical training, but it was, to start with, a native and direct curiosity about everybody. Later, as I will show, this basic democratic feeling in her developed not into political theory but into a sort of secular saintliness.

So "the good Anna" is first of all a human type, living and dying as that type does. She is presented first not as a child or a young girl but in her full development, in a situation which gives full expression to her typical kind of force, which is incessant managing will. The first chapter gives her as the type of that, the second chapter gives her life, and the third chapter her death. It is a curious kind of construction, which derives from "Un Coeur Simple." Flaubert begins: "Pendant un demi-siècle, les bourgeois de Pont-L'Evêque envièrent à Mme Aubain sa servante Félicité. Pour cent francs par an, elle faisait la cuisine et le ménage, cousait, lavait, repassait, savait brider un cheval, engraisser les volailles, battre le beurre, et resta fidèle à sa maitresse,—qui cependant n'était pas une personne agréable." After this summary presentation Flaubert goes on to recount assorted episodes demonstrating Félicité's courage, loyalty, generosity, affection, etc. "Elle avait eu, comme une autre, son histoire d'amour." "The Good Anna" begins: "The tradesmen of Bridgepoint learned to dread the sound of 'Miss Mathilda,' for with that name the good Anna always conquered." And later: "The widow Mrs. Lehntman was the romance in Anna's life."

Now while the situations and episodes in "The Good Anna" are chosen and arranged to show the character of the subject in various relationships, the qualities of the character are not primarily moral. The word "good," which is repeated as constantly as a Homeric epithet before the name Anna, does not indicate an evaluation of the character or a conclusion about it but the constantly present essence of the character which is there as a fact and not as a value. Like the word "poor" which is used of Anna, Melanctha, and Lena, it gives a rather perfunctory general shape to the character, like the terribly simple shape of a Cézanne head or apple. Both the epithet and the shape of the apple look awkward and crude from the point of view of more graceful and less serious art, say that of Whistler or Pater, but these raw simplicities are necessary to hold down or stabilize an extreme complexity of interrelationship. It is like the melodrama of Henry James. Not to press these parallels too far, but as the Cézanne apple has weight and existence not by its shape or by perspective but by an equilibrium of relationships within the space of the picture, so the good Anna gets weight and existence, almost as a physical consistency, from her relationships within the account.

Anna found her place with large, abundant women, for such were always lazy, careless or all helpless, and so the burden of their lives could fall on Anna, and give her just content. Anna's superiors must be always these large helpless women, or be men, for none others could give themselves to be made so comfortable and free.

Anna had no strong natural feeling to love children, as she had to love cats and dogs, and a large mistress. She never became deeply fond of Edgar and Jane Wadsmith. She naturally preferred the boy, for boys love always better to be done for and made comfortable and full of eating, while in

30

the little girl she had to meet the feminine, the subtle opposi-
tion, showing so early always in a young girl's nature.[4]

*Miss Mary was sitting in a large armchair by the fire. All
the nooks and crannies of the chair were filled full of her
soft and spreading body. She was dressed in a black satin
morning gown, the sleeves, great monster things, were heavy
with the mass of her soft flesh. She sat there always, large,
helpless, gentle. She had a fair, soft, regular, good-looking
face, with pleasant, empty, grey-blue eyes, and heavy sleepy
lids.*

*Behind Miss Mary was the little Jane, nervous and jerky
with excitement as she saw Anna come into the room.*

*"Miss Mary," Anna began. She had stopped just within
the door, her body and her face stiff with repression, her
teeth closed hard and the white lights flashing sharply in
the pale, clean blue of her eyes. Her bearing was full of the
strange coquetry of anger and of fear, the stiffness, the bri-
dling, the suggestive movement underneath the rigidity of
forced control, all the queer ways the passions have to show
themselves all one.*

*"Miss Mary," the words came slowly with thick utterance
and with jerks, but always firm and strong. "Miss Mary, I
can't stand it any more like this. When you tell me anything
to do, I do it. I do everything I can and you know I work
myself sick for you. The blue dressings in your room makes
too much work to have for summer. Miss Jane don't know
what work is. If you want to do things like that I go away."*

*Anna stopped still. Her words had not the strength of
meaning they were meant to have, but the power in the mood
of Anna's soul frightened and awed Miss Mary through and
through.*

*Like in all large and helpless women, Miss Mary's heart
beat weakly in the soft and helpless mass it had to govern.*

4. *Three Lives* (Modern Library, 1933), p. 25.

31

Little Jane's excitements had already tried her strength. Now she grew pale and fainted quite away.[5]

This last scene is as an event no more than a slapstick episode. It comes from a gift Gertrude Stein had and never lost, for extremely broad and reckless farce. In this same story she distinguishes two varieties or gradations of it.

"Her freakish humor now first showed itself, her sense of fun in the queer ways that people had, that made her later find delight in brutish servile Katy, in Sally's silly ways and in the badness of Peter and of Rags." [6]

"Anna always had a humorous sense from this old Katy's twisted peasant english, from the roughness on her tongue of buzzing s's and from the queer ways of her servile brutish humor." [7]

As the passions are all one the humor is all one through its gradations, and very much continuous with Gertrude Stein. She had an extraordinary mimetic faculty that allowed her not only to take on the full nature of her subject—in this case to the point of composing her episode in the manner of her characters—but to follow the gradations of a theme or feeling into its farthest and faintest developments. For example the character of dogs becomes quite comparable to the character of people, and this not sentimentally or metaphorically but as the brain of a dog can be studied with the human brain and is not very different.

And then Peter never strayed away, and he looked out of his nice eyes and he liked it when you rubbed him down, and he forgot you when you went away, and he barked whenever there was any noise.

When he was a little pup he had one night been put into

5. *Ibid.*, pp. 28–29.
6. *Ibid.*, pp. 37–38.
7. *Ibid.*, p. 17.

the yard and that was all of his origin she knew. The good Anna loved him well and spoiled him as a good german mother always does her son.

Little Rags was very different in his nature. He was a lively creature made out of ends of things, all fluffy and dust color, and he was always bounding up into the air and darting all about over and then under silly Peter and often straight into solemn fat, blind, sleepy Baby, and then in a wild rush after some stray cat.

Rags was a pleasant, jolly little fellow. The good Anna liked him very well, but never with her strength as she loved her good looking coward, foolish young man, Peter.

Baby was the dog of her past life and she held Anna with old ties of past affection. Peter was the spoiled, good looking young man, of her middle age, and Rags was always something of a toy. She liked him but he never struck in very deep.[8]

Gertrude Stein is here dealing with broad classifications or types of character and relationship, minutely distinguished and identified. The scientific accuracy or the accuracy of intuition very consciously overrides the inaccuracies of common sense which would say one's feelings about a dog have little or no relation to one's feelings about a person. The humor of this kind of paradox, a rather broad sympathetic irony, is, as I suggested, the pervading tone of this work. The same irony carries the scene with Miss Mary, where the event is broad to the point of vulgarity, but where the feelings involved are distinguished and identified with great finesse. This intricate and accurate elaboration of the broad, the normal, the commonplace, is a method she used all her life. It is at once American and classical, as I will try to show much later.

She was trained to a very sharp scalpel and there is a medi-

8. *Ibid.,* p. 68.

cal neatness about how Miss Mary fills her chair and Anna's being just inside the door. It is a somewhat forced neatness of contour as one finds it in Cézanne and in Flaubert, in Juan Gris. With Gertrude Stein it is, among other things, a sort of feminine daintiness that can become a fussiness now and then, and that can work either as an irritation or a personal charm on the reader. But here it makes very clear the constant definition of Anna's character by the description of its functions in a variety of relationships. For closer and closer definition and distinction the terms naturally have to be very simple, if it is all going to be clear. The terms of the definition or expression are used in as absolute a sense as may be. In the sentence "The tradesmen of Bridgepoint learned to dread the sound of 'Miss Mathilda,' for with that name the good Anna always conquered" the word "conquered" is used absolutely. It is *le mot juste* with a vengeance. It does not depend, for the expression of the present subject, on connotations of Alexander the Great or Cortez. It is used in its essential or axiomatic meaning of succeeding and dominating in an enterprise against resistance. It is used without historical resonance and suggestion, without, so to speak, the conventional perspective of literary language. To some extent, in this early work, it may play *against* conventional perspective, as the relational depth in Cézanne seems to play paradoxically against traditional perspective, but that paradox is a secondary interest. As with Cézanne, the new usage stands by itself as solid and accurate, without reference to what it contradicts. The verbal irony here, such as it may be, is only a minor distraction, at most an incidental reflection of the larger and more serious irony at the heart of the work. At any rate, she relied less and less on the rather cosmetic interest of verbal irony, and made no apologies for absolute and categorical meaning. This was directly against another contemporary movement, of composition by the multiplication of resonances and ambiguities.

34

If the character then is defined by its relationships and its consistency of force, there is the question of presentation. The narrative becomes episodic, as I have explained, and there are plenty of flat statements, generalities, and discourses. That is, the *presentation* does still rely on demonstration and even on explanation. But the really extraordinary thing about the good Anna is that the character is thought of also as a musical continuity. Already in Radcliffe Gertrude Stein had described the conflict between the conscious and the automatic parts of her subjects in experiments as being like two themes going on together in music, one and the other dominating alternately. This and the opera may have been the beginning of the idea. Solomons noted that her attention was mainly auditory,[9] and she herself speaks of doing a great deal of listening then, not to what was being said so much as to the way it was being said, the rise and fall, and the characteristic variety of emphasis. She used to call this "the rhythm of a personality." The phrase sounds now like a rather fancy affectation, but it had an exact and responsible meaning within what was being thought about human psychology at the time. It was not rhythm for pleasure in rhythm but a thing existing in the living personality that could be accurately registered and described. The means for registering this was inevitably the language as spoken or as written. In *Three Lives* this is conveyed clearly enough in the dialogue parts. There is a handsome example of this projection by rhythm in dialogue in a scene between the good Anna and Mrs. Lehntman.

"I know you was careless, Mrs. Lehntman, but I didn't think that you could do this so. No, Mrs. Lehntman, it ain't your duty to take up with no others, when you got two children of your own, that got to get along just any way they can, and you know you ain't got any too much money all the time, and

9. *Psychological Review*, III (1896), No. 5, 500.

you are all so careless here and spend it all the time, and Julia and Willie growin' big. It ain't right, Mrs. Lehntman, to do so."

This was as bad as it could be. Anna had never spoken her mind so to her friend before. . . . And then too Mrs. Lehntman could not really take in harsh ideas. She was too well diffused to catch the feel of any sharp firm edge.

Now she managed to understand all this in a way that made it easy for her to say, "Why, Anna, I think you feel too bad about seeing what the children are doing every minute in the day. Julia and Willie are real good, and they play with all the nicest children in the square. . . . No indeed Anna, it's easy enough to say I should send this poor, cute little boy to a 'sylum when I could keep him here so nice, but you know Anna, you wouldn't like to do it yourself, now you really know you wouldn't, Anna, though you talk to me so hard.— My, it's hot to-day, what you doin' with that ice tea in there Julia, when Miss Annie is waiting all this time for her drink?"

Julia brought in the ice tea. . . .

"Here Miss Annie," Julia said, "Here, Miss Annie, is your glass of tea, I know you like it good and strong."

"No, Julia, I don't want no ice tea here. Your mamma ain't able to afford now using her money upon ice tea for her friends. It ain't right she should now any more. . . ."

"My, Miss Annie is real mad now," Julia said, as the house shook, as the good Anna shut the outside door with a concentrated shattering slam.[10]

In this passage the hard rage of Anna, the bland diffusion of Mrs. Lehntman, and the nasty silliness of Julia are conveyed by the rhythm of the talk I think very well. But in prose, since there can be no explicit indication of staccato or legato or speed or *dolce*, the exact phrasing can easily be lost by the reader. Gertrude Stein supplies some direction,

10. *Three Lives*, pp. 44–45.

not only from the natural assumptions of the scene but by such words as sharp, firm, hard, and then for Mrs. Lehntman, diffused, easy. With these directions one can so to speak interpret the piece fairly accurately. But the rhythm involves much more than the matters of beat and phrasing and metrics. The physical verbal rhythm is in itself relatively simple and heavy, like the vocabulary. It would correspond to say a simple ¾ time in comparison to the elaborate syncopations and runs and glides and suspensions of late 19th century prose, or poetry—or to the palette of Cézanne as against an infinitely graduated impressionist palette, say that of Monet. But as with the vocabulary, the simplification of the rhythm is there to carry and clarify something complicated. Very much as, in the experiment I quoted at length in the first chapter, a metronome controlled the succession of meaningless syllables, as a condition for the functioning of the attention in memorizing, so here the functioning of the attention of the characters in speech (which would be according to Gertrude Stein's early definition a reflex of their total character) goes on against a simplified verbal rhythm. It has to be simple to disengage the special personal emphasis and to carry a rhythm of ideas. By a rhythm of ideas I mean only that as anyone goes on talking, or as we say expressing himself, there is in the sequence and force of the things said a very definite rate of change and a pattern of recurrence. The rate of change is largely a matter of the duration of interest, or as we would say the attention span, or as they said at Radcliffe a pulse beat of consciousness, quickened or sluggish. This is much more natural than it sounds. In the 19th century novel the thing said expresses the character insofar as it shows an attitude or, in Aristotle's word, a predilection. What a man has to say about his mother, about foreigners, about the new wing to the rectory expresses his character. We get not the essence of the character in process so much as little incidents or lights about the character. After

37

an accumulation of them one can feel the character is all there and alive, that one knows what to expect of him in any little action. The patter passages of Jane Austen, Trollope, and Dickens do go beyond this, to presenting the mind of the character in process directly, but it all tends to be crippled by the conventions of current grammar and literary style or dialect, or obstructed by material furthering the plot or the atmosphere or the philosophy.

In the passage quoted above and in the scene with Miss Mary quoted earlier, the ideas expressed have hardly any personal idiosyncrasy, they are in themselves the bleakest commonplaces, and this neutrality serves as a foil to make clear the extremely delicate sequence and emphasis of the ideas as they come out of the character in accordance with the vital intensity and frequency of that character. The ideas of the enraged Anna come with a steady insistence as well as abrupt change. Consider how the pressure that has to be put not only on the metric but on the meaning of the phrase "to do so" expresses the violence in Anna more directly than external description or greater eloquence of vocabulary and idea. The repetition of the name Mrs. Lehntman is Anna's way of making the woman stay there and hold still under the pounding reproaches. The use of the word "here" in the phrase "and you are all so careless here and spend it all the the time" is again a way of arresting the household for the attack. The repetition of the phrase "all the time" is again a way of enveloping their behavior for total condemnation. In contrast the charming "easy" maundering expostulation of Mrs. Lehntman dwells softly on irrelevances until the final incoherence of calling for the ice tea. Gertrude Stein says earlier, "It was wonderful how Mrs. Lehntman could listen and not hear, could answer and yet not decide, could say and do what she was asked and yet leave things as they were before." [11]

11. *Ibid.*, p. 39.

This differs from the method of Proust. With him the peculiarities of speech, the curious idiom of vocabulary, both verbal and ideal, all project the precise social or historical coloring of the character. Not that drama and an expressive rhythm are not in it, but they are not disengaged from an extremely complex harmonics in every phrase uttered by Françoise or Charlus, for example. Gertrude Stein reduces the tonality, the pedal, and disengages the pure melody and rhythm. We are out of Wagner say into Satie. This is one part of what she called the destruction of associational emotion.

In "The Good Anna" she tries numerous other methods for presenting the characters alive, besides direct dialogue. One attempt is to run Anna's abrupt rhythm across the dialogue into the narrative: " 'Peter!,'—her voice rose higher,—'Peter!,' —Peter was the youngest and the favorite dog,—'Peter if you don't leave Baby alone,'—Baby was an old, blind terrier that Anna had loved for many years,—'Peter if you don't leave Baby alone, I take a rawhide to you, you bad dog.' " [12] The consistency corresponding to the rhythm is given in physical descriptions: "At this time Anna, about twenty-seven years of age, was not yet all thin and worn. The sharp bony edges and corners of her head and face were still rounded out with flesh, but already the temper and the humor showed sharply in her clean blue eyes, and the thinning was begun about the lower jaw, that was so often strained with the upward pressure of resolve." [13] The quality of incessant strain and pressure, Anna's particular quality, pervades nearly everything in the story, from the structure and transitions to the least matters of style. It is, like the work of Flaubert, exhaustively coordinated. It seems all to be written on the signature as it were of one of the earliest sentences: "Anna led an arduous and troubled life."

12. *Ibid.*, p. 12.
13. *Ibid.*, p. 28.

Whatever this analysis may make it look like, "The Good Anna" is not merely an exercise in technique, though certainly very brilliant as an exercise. The story comes really from a simple animal necessity to express something living. It is more a matter of feeling than philosophy that decides that remarks about people or the story of what happened to them does not adequately or directly express them living. It takes a very vivid, even rank sense of life and a great intellectual vitality not to sacrifice the intuition of the living to the inadequate but accepted form, and then to use all available means and inventions to express that living as truly as one can. "The Good Anna" is an effort to do so.

But the impact and influence of *Three Lives* were mainly by its verbal novelty. It destroyed the extenuated rhetoric of the late 19th century. Wordsworth and the romantics had broken up the late classical rhetoric and regulated the written language on the natural idiom or on personal impulse. Language, like people, put off the perruque and wore an open collar. But the complex and ineffable longings of the natural life became standardized into attitudes, Byronic and others, and the language settled into as perfunctory a rhetoric as the classical. It wound up as art for art. And people did their hair correspondingly, making necessary the antimacassar. Then Gertrude Stein inevitably came to the crew cut.

Three Lives, more radically than any other work of the time in English, brought the language back to life. Not the life of the peasantry or the emotions or the proletariat but life as it was lived by anybody living in the century, the average or normal life as the naturalists had seen it. Gertrude Stein in this work tried to coordinate the composition of the language with the process of consciousness, which, we have seen, was to her a close reflex of the total living personality. If this was to be done at least two serious things had to happen to the language:

First the word had to have not its romantic or literary

40

meaning but the immediate meaning it had to the contemporary using it, a literal axiomatic meaning confined to the simple situations of the average life. The heroines of *Three Lives*, two German women and a Negress, have no connection whatever with the literary past of the language. The words are not used either as the authentic dialect of Baltimore Germans or Negroes; rather the perfunctory dialect convention serves as a pretext for liberating the language from literary convention.

The second necessity was to destroy 19th century syntax and word order, which could not follow the movement of a consciousness moving naturally, this movement being, in the early 20th century, of the utmost importance. Gertrude Stein had read a great deal of Elizabethan prose and poetry, in particular the prose of Robert Greene, and to that extent had a precedent and model for an extremely loose syntax which could follow the immediate interest and impulse of the consciousness, whether lively and extravagant or simply ruminant. The prose of Greene is normally full of the rather swaggering rapid movement and brutal emphasis of his person.[14] The prose and construction of "The Good Anna" are based on something of the same quality in the character of the heroine.

As Whitman for example had destroyed 19th century metrics and verse forms, Gertrude Stein destroyed 19th century syntax and word order. Her work at this is comparable to what G. M. Hopkins was doing with syntax in his poetry, but there is a very great difference between them. Hopkins had as a Jesuit a casuist training in very fine distinctions of

14. Greene, in his tract on Coney-catching, claimed a propriety (even $\tau\grave{o}$ $\pi\rho\acute{\epsilon}\pi o\nu$) in using a plain style for a low subject. This fact is historically curious but entirely unimportant. His appeal to a classical theory in fashion is a casual justification of a much more important thing, his perfectly direct undecorated literal vision of the subject. Gertrude Stein always admired this tradition, through Defoe and Trollope.

idea, a training corresponding considerably to the medical and philosophical training of Gertrude Stein. But, and I believe this is important, Hopkins was a straight baroque poet. The baroque style [15] is equivalent to the Jesuit style, none too roughly, and they are both creations of the Counter Reformation, motivated by a desire to keep an escaping thing under. Under authority or under a formula or under the intellect or under the eye, it does not much matter. The baroque means, as a conquest, to bring everything under a closed system and within reach of the authorities. ("Glory be to God for dappled things.") The tension of the baroque is simply that struggle, heroic or sometimes just frantic. In the time of Hopkins the religious motive happened to coincide with a similar motive on the part of 19th century science and also the British Empire. All in all it leads to a closed and finished art, the stuffing of something inside something else, even if it wrenches the container considerably. Joyce, in the 20th century, went on with this, cramming everything into the scheme of the *Odyssey* or cyclic time, so that one may say that he was the last hypertrophy of the 19th century and destroyed it by overdoing it.

The early work of Gertrude Stein is still rather haunted by the pretention to universal inclusion, not of Catholicism of course but of naturalistic or evolutionary science. *The Making of Americans* is a universal history of human types and *Three Lives* has the paradigmatic force of naturalist writing. But the form and method and intent differ greatly from the insular Catholic product. The virtue of that product is to

15. "The baroque" can of course be more generally defined as the collision of the romantic with the classical, their struggle or their embrace on about equal terms. I do not think it should be carried beyond that to mean any mixture, however unequal, of the classic and romantic, because that would ultimately include everything. In any event, I use the term here in its ordinary sense, to mean the baroque par excellence, that of the 16th and 17th centuries, and later styles organized on virtually the same grounds.

re-create the corporeal presence of everything within its little room, but the art of Gertrude Stein, being not insular but continental, is, even so early, generalized and disembodied, representing rather than including the totality of cases by single simple axioms. The form itself makes an enclosure, but this, as a reflection of a theory of consciousness, does not stand as a receptacle but as a field of activity, "a space of time that is filled always filled with moving." [16] Otherwise her work, like that of Whitman, is all wide open spaces. It is absolutely not institutional or sectarian, it cannot be cathartic or tragic or salvationist, it is not out to justify or condemn or set things right. She had, to a startling degree, no sense of alienation from the universe but took it as a miraculously given thing. She speaks somewhere of the daily miracle that happens to the artist. The religious parallel to this very secular art would be not doctrine or ritual or institution but arbitrarily the state of grace. She teased everyone by calling this her being a genius. She was, I have no doubt, but the importance of that for the reader is not in the value but in the orientation it gives her work.

"The Good Anna," as pioneer work, does have its uncertainties and imperfections. I do not see how, for example, it is not a mistake to use the word "nay," or to mention the Struldbrugs, or to speak of "the dust which settles with the ages." But if these are errors they are errors with a meaning. They take up the prophetic tone of voice used loudly enough by Whitman, Melville, and later Hart Crane and Wolfe, to carry over the wide open spaces. In the case of Gertrude Stein it is the first appearance of the sibylline manner [17] that is found in a great deal of her later work, where it perfectly belongs.

16. *Lectures in America* (Random House, 1935), p. 161.
17. Barring of course the daily themes she wrote at Radcliffe. The magniloquence of many passages in the themes is a combination of George Eliot's influence, youth, and very likely a deliberate flouting of New England reticence.

The third story of *Three Lives*, "The Gentle Lena," contains no great novelty beyond "The Good Anna." It is in a way a pendant to the first story in that Lena is a study of a soft and fluid and even absent consciousness and character as against the emphatic and hard presence of Anna. "Lena was patient, gentle, sweet and german." It is a delicious little story and prettily turned. It at least shows that Gertrude Stein was even this early capable of grace and easy elegance in the midst of her revolution. Further, it has a simple tenderness within complete clarity which so far as I know is unique in our literature. The nearest thing to it would be Sherwood Anderson.

But according to the general agreement the big thing in *Three Lives* is the middle story, "Melanctha." It is a tragic love story ending in death from consumption, so that it is available to the traditional literary taste and the educated emotions. Furthermore it is, as Carl Van Vechten says, "perhaps the first American story in which the Negro is regarded as a human being and not as an object for condescending compassion or derision." [18] It is a good deal to have attained that clarity and equilibrium of feeling in a difficult question, but "Melanctha" as a piece of literature does much more.

Where "The Good Anna" and "The Gentle Lena" are composed as the presentation of a single type in illustrative incidents, Melanctha is composed on the dramatic trajectory of a passion. If "The Good Anna" roughly corresponds to "Un Coeur Simple," "Melanctha" corresponds roughly to *Madame Bovary*. Very roughly, and there is most likely no direct influence, but it makes an illuminating comparison.

Madame Bovary and the course of her passion are presented in an elaborate series of incidents, situations, landscapes, interiors, extraneous issues; in short they are measured and realized against a thick objective context as the things in the context are measured against her desire.

18. Preface, *Three Lives*, p. x.

Strangely enough this desire is never directly presented. It is measured somewhat by its casual source in her romantic reading—as Don Quijote is casually accounted for by his reading of the romances of chivalry—and it is known later by its various objects such as travel in far lands, luxuries, poetry written to her, and so on. As a blind desire, and probably as a death wish, it is symbolized by the awful blind beggar who is as it were Emma's *Doppelgänger* and who is finally put out of the way by Homais, the type of cheap rationalism. Emma's power is measured again by her being too much for Charles, for Léon, and even for Rodolphe, and by the pathetic infatuation of the boy Justin. She has certainly a variety of states of mind, wild desire, remorse, boredom, religiosity, fear, and so on, but they are a succession of distinct states, presented as complete and not as in process. In brief, Flaubert's art was spatial and intensely pictorial, not temporal and musical. Expressing directly and exactly the immediate movement, pulse, and process of a thing simply was not his business. But it was in this early period Gertrude Stein's business, and in "Melanctha" she did express at length the process of a passion.

She did not yet disengage the essential vitality entirely from its natural context. There are some few descriptions of railroad yards, docks, country scenes, houses, yards, rooms, windows, but these are reduced to a telling minimum. There is also some accounting for the complex forces in the heroine's character by the brutality of her father and the sweet indifference of her mother. She is described at the beginning of the story by contrast and association with Rose Johnson, her hard-headed decent friend, and again by the same contrast enlarged at the end of the story, when Rose casts her off. But the real demonstration of the story is the dialogue between Melanctha and her lover Jeff Campbell. In this long dialogue, which is like a duel or duet, the traditional incoherence between the inner and the outer life has been replaced by an incoherence between two subjectivities. It is conceived of as a difference in tempo, the slow Jeff against the quick Melanctha.[19] Also there is already very much present in this story the difference, the radical and final difference in people, defined in *The Making of Americans* as the attacking and the resisting kinds or types. It is not quite the difference between active and passive, as both kinds are based on a persistence in being or in living, and they are further complicated by a deviousness and modulation in function. For example, how does a naturally attacking kind resist and how does a naturally resisting kind get provoked to attack? All this is elaborately and dramatically worked out in the long dialogue. "It was a struggle, sure to be going on always between them. It was a struggle that was as sure always to be going on between them, as their minds and hearts always were to have different ways of working." [20] Their differences, shade by shade, and their gradual reconciliations are presented through the whole course of the affair from indifference to gradual fascination to the struggle for domination by a variety of means, to the decline into brotherly and sisterly affection, and finally to the final break.

Gertrude Stein had already, in a story written in 1903 and called *Quod Erat Demonstrandum* but not published until 1950 and under the title *Things as They Are*,[21] worked out a very similar dialectic of a passion. It is very interesting as a preliminary exercise for "Melanctha." As its first title sug-

19. This conception, of tempo of character as the cardinal difficulty in a love story, is already distinct if not developed in her Radcliffe theme of December 29, 1894. (See Rosalind S. Miller, *Gertrude Stein: Form and Intelligibility* [Exposition Press, 1949], p. 124.) This theme, entitled "The Great Enigma," is no doubt drawn from a real episode, and the conception of character probably rose directly out of experience, not out of other literature or the psychological laboratory, though this last surely verified and developed the idea.

20. *Three Lives*, p. 153.

21. Banyan Press, 1950.

gests, it is an intensive and exhaustive study of relations in a triangle. In its way it is a Jamesian study or demonstration, and its heroine mentions and quotes the heroine and/or villainess of James' novel *The Wings of the Dove*, Kate Croy. But *Things as They Are* bears a more striking resemblance to the *Adolphe* of Benjamin Constant, it has the same merciless directness and concentration, and though Gertrude Stein had probably not read *Adolphe* in 1903 this earliest work belongs to the tradition of *Adolphe* and of *La Princesse de Clèves*. It has the same unwavering intellectual clarity applied to the perpetually shifting relationships of a passion throughout its course. That much is already mastered in this first work, but the handling tends more to commentary than to presentation and has not the sure grasp of the personal cadences of a character's thought and feeling that makes the analyses in "Melanctha" a direct expression of character in movement. This is partly the fault of the characters themselves in *Things as They Are*. They are white American college women, whose speech and thought are bound to be at odds with their feeling. Gertrude Stein treats this difficulty handsomely enough as subject matter, but the expressive power of the prose is limited by its very propriety to the subject matter. It is very pure, immensely intelligent, and astonishing for a first work in 1903, but it is polite, cultivated, educated, literary. Compare with the passage from "Melanctha," quoted above, the following from *Things as They Are*:

"Time passed and they renewed their habit of desultory meetings at public places, but these were not the same as before. There was between them now a consciousness of strain, a sense of new adjustments, of uncertain standards and of changing values." [22]

"Melanctha," in which the characters are Negroes, has thereby the advantage of "uneducated" speech, and of a direct relationship between feeling and word, a more funda-

22. *Things as They Are*, p. 30.

mental or universal drama. It is a measure of her strength that in making the most of the advantage Gertrude Stein abandoned polite or cultivated writing completely and forever, so completely that the press where she had *Three Lives* printed sent to inquire if she really knew English.

At all events, "Melanctha" is, as I said the work of Henry James was, a time continuum less of events than of considerations of their meaning. The events considered in "Melanctha" are mostly the movements of the passion, how Jeff and Melanctha feel differently toward each other from moment to moment.

Like the characters of James, Melanctha and Jeff are preternaturally articulate about their feelings, but where James keeps the plausibilities by using highly cultivated characters to express the complicated meaning in an endless delicacy of phrasing, Gertrude Stein uses the simplest possible words, the common words used by everybody, and a version of the most popular phrasing, to express the very complicated thing. It is true and exciting that James often used the simplest possible word for his complicated meaning, but he had a tendency to isolate it to the attention, to force it to carry its full weight by printing it in italics or putting it in quotes, or dislocating it from its more usual place in the word order, or repeating it. Gertrude Stein uses repetition and dislocation to make the word bear all the meaning it has, but actually one has to give her work word by word the deliberate attention one gives to something written in italics. It has been said that her work means more when one reads it in proof or very slowly, and that is certainly true, the work has to be read word by word, as a succession of single meanings accumulating into a larger meaning, as for example the words in the stanza of a song being sung. Unhappily all our training and most of our reasons for reading are against this. Very likely the desire for simplicity in style is most often a desire that the words and ideas along the way to the formu-

48

lated conclusion, the point, be perfectly negligible and that we have no anxious feeling we are missing anything as we rush by. But as an example of how Gertrude Stein forces the simplest negligible words to stay there in a full meaning:

"Can't you understand Melanctha, ever, how no man certainly ever really can hold your love for long times together. You certainly Melanctha, you ain't got down deep loyal feeling, true inside you, and when you ain't just that moment quick with feeling, then you certainly ain't ever got anything more there to keep you. You see Melanctha, it certainly is this way with you, it is, that you ain't ever got any way to remember right what you been doing, or anybody else that has been feeling with you. You certainly Melanctha, never can remember right, when it comes what you have done and what you think happens to you." "It certainly is all easy for you Jeff Campbell to be talking. You remember right, because you don't remember nothing till you get home with your thinking everything all over, but I certainly don't think much ever of that kind of way of remembering right, Jeff Campbell. I certainly do call it remembering right Jeff Campbell, to remember right just when it happens to you, so you have a right kind of feeling not to act the way you always been doing to me, and then you go home Jeff Campbell, and you begin with your thinking, and then it certainly is very easy for you to be good and forgiving with it. No, that ain't to me, the way of remembering Jeff Campbell, not as I can see it not to make people always suffer, waiting for you certainly to get to do it. . . ." [23]

The passage is, if one likes, about the synchronization of feeling upon the present activity. Anyone can see what is meant by the argument if the feeling discussed is understood to be sexual feeling. But the thing which makes this

23. *Three Lives*, pp. 180–181.

passage absolutely accurate and not euphemistic is that the subject is literally feeling, all feeling, inasmuch as all the passions are one. In brief, making abstraction of objects and situations, sexual feeling behaves no differently from other feelings. The readiness, slowness, concentration or absent-mindedness, domination or dependence in sexual feeling are about the same as in all the other activities of a character. So that we have here a perfect propriety and fullness of diction.

The relatively simple dislocations of "you ain't got down deep loyal feeling, true inside you," from the more common-place order "you have no true feeling of loyalty deep down inside you," not only jar the words awake into their full mean-ing but follow with much greater exactitude the slow, pas-sionate, clumsy emphasis of Jeff Campbell's feeling.

The phrase "remembering right" could be replaced by a more familiar cliché, "profiting aptly by past experience," or by scientific gabble like "the coordination of habitual reflexes upon the present object," but the advantage of the simpler new phrase is that it expresses the matter in terms of the fundamental and final activities and categories of the mind. It is part of the "impulse to elemental abstraction," the description in terms of the final and generic as against description by context and association. It is like the generi-cally round and sitting apple of Cézanne as against a deli-cately compromised and contextuated and reverberating apple of the impressionists. The propriety of the simple popular abstraction used in "Melanctha" is in this, that the two subjectivities at odds are seen, and so to be described, directly—directly from common knowledge, and not, as with *Madame Bovary*, seen refracted and described indirectly through an exterior context embodying considerable special knowledge. The immediate terms of *Madame Bovary* are saturated with French history, the immediate terms of "Me-lanctha" are the final categories of mental process—to know,

50

to see, to hear, to wish, to remember, to suffer, and the like.

However, "Melanctha" is more than an exact chart of the passions. The conjugation or play of the abstractions proceeds according to the vital rhythm or tempo of the characters. In this way the essential quality of the characters is not only described but presented immediately. As Emma Bovary is *seen* against the rake Rodolphe and then against the pusillanimous Léon, and is thereby defined, so Melanctha is, in her quick tempo, *played* against the slow Jeff Campbell and then against the very fast "dashing" Jem Richards.

Gertrude Stein later made some remarks about *Three Lives* in the light of her later problems of expression. In *Composition as Explanation* she said:

In beginning writing I wrote a book called Three Lives *this was written in 1905. I wrote a negro story called* Melanctha. *In that there was a constant recurring and beginning there was a marked direction in the direction of being in the present although naturally I had been accustomed to past present and future, and why, because the composition forming around me was a prolonged present. A composition of a prolonged present is a natural composition in the world as it has been these thirty years [1926] it was more and more a prolonged present. I created then a prolonged present naturally I knew nothing of a continuous present but it came naturally to me to make one, it was simple it was clear to me and nobody knew why it was done like that, I did not myself although naturally to me it was natural. . . .*

In the first book [Three Lives] *there was a groping for a continuous present and for using everything by beginning again and again.*[24]

The difference between a prolonged and a continuous present may be defined as this, that a prolonged present as-

24. *Composition as Explanation* (Hogarth Press, 1926), pp. 16–17, 18.

51

sumes a situation or a theme and dwells on it and develops it or keeps it recurring, as in much opera, and Bach, for example. The continuous present would take each successive moment or passage as a completely new thing essentially, as with Mozart or Scarlatti or, later, Satie. This Gertrude Stein calls beginning again. But the problem is really one of the dimensions of the present as much as of the artist's way with it. The "specious" present which occupied William James is an arbitrary distinction between past and future as they flow together in time. But for purposes of action and art it has to be assumed as an operable space of time. For the composer this space of time can be the measure, or whatever unit can be made to express something without dependence on succession as the condition of its interest. For the writer it can be the sentence or the paragraph or the chapter or the scene or the page or the stanza or whatever. Gertrude Stein experimented with all these units in the course of her work, but in the early work the struggle was mainly with the sentence and the paragraph.

2.

The next book, the enormous one, *The Making of Americans*, has been explained at some length by Gertrude Stein in the lecture called "The Gradual Making of the Making of Americans," and also in *Composition as Explanation*, but still something more can be said, in particular about its place with her other work.

Compared with *Three Lives*, it is far more disembodied, both from physical description and from dramatic story. Where the abstracted interiority of Melanctha was seen in dramatic relation to the interiority of Jeff Campbell, the people in *The Making of Americans* are seen as an enormous collection of separate units with almost no active relation to each other. They are fathers, mothers, sons, and daughters well enough, but this is, *to themselves inside them* and to the presentation, a fairly adventitious situation or quality to their separate interior existences. They are always young men and women to themselves, not children or old people; the quality of being a son or an uncle does not depend at all on the specific parents or nephews and nieces who objectively create the position. The individual people in the book go on and on as themselves, schematically situated in family relationships which do or do not have meaning to them. As living beings, as verbs, they are intransitive, and they tend also to be present participles: "Many having resisting being have it in them all their living when they are beginning and then on to their ending have it to have suspicion always naturally in them and this is a natural thing for them to have in them because they have resisting being have it in them to be knowing that always someone is doing attacking." [25]

All these separate individuals are related mainly to a few essential classifications developed by Gertrude Stein—the attacking type and the resisting type, the *dependent independent* type and the *independent dependent* type. These final types serve as coordinates for the exact charting of particular characters, or as absolute black and white can serve to measure the tone of any color. Every possible character can be placed within these coordinates. They give the external coherence and the scope to a book which was projected as the history of "everyone who ever was or is or will be living."

That sounds like too much—a history of the future, indeed—but it is quite accurate. Any history assumes a plane of relevance for the presentation of the material, whether the plane be political, economic, military, dramatic, biographical, or moral. The irrelevant is ignored, though it was, as a matter of fact, there. One does not give the private history of every soldier at the Battle of Waterloo. One can give

25. *The Making of Americans*, in *Selected Writings*, p. 274.

a sample of such a thing, as Stendhal and Tolstoi did it. But Fabrice and Pierre do not behave in battle any differently than they behave in other circumstances, and if the characters are taken as the historical facts, the Battle of the Berezina or the Battle of Waterloo has no meaning except as an example, as a demonstration rather than as a fact. *The Making of Americans*, being a history of people and not of events, very rarely uses events, even to demonstrate character. The characters are not, as in most traditional history, situated in relation to external events, to war and peace, to progress and reaction, to the formation and decline of national cultures (in spite of the title), or just the ambience of contemporary gossip, but to their ultimate ways of being alive in and to the universe—attacking or resisting, dependence or independence.

But naturally the primary dimension of history is time. From Herodotus on, the historiographical sense of objective time and sequence, measured by years or battles or epochs, has been in constant change. It is a long and quite interesting story, but by the 19th century the sense of objective time was ripe and beginning to decay. History was getting philosophized and mythologized. At any rate the notion of subjective time was completely clear by the beginning of the 20th century. Proust is the clearest demonstration of biography written in subjective, not objective, time. *The Making of Americans* is a history written in subjective time. It is not the sequence of events and years but, if you like, the stream of consciousness.

As I said in the first chapter it makes a difference if one conceives a stream of consciousness or a stream of thought, that is, a continuous receptivity or a continuous activity of conception. Allowing certainly for his analytical gift and his splendors of construction, the presented continuity in Proust is a continuity of perception, of registration, like the surface of an impressionist painting; while in *The Making of Ameri-*

cans the continuity is one of conception, of constant activity in terms of the mind and not the senses and emotions, like the surface of a cubist painting. This stream of thought is naturally the stream of Gertrude Stein's thought, and is very simply assumed as the final reality. This does not make it a subjective history in the sense of being private or a matter of capricious opinion. The work itself, the sequence of statements and ideas, makes the stream of thought perfectly objective and available to anyone who can read English. And the material is not highly special and idiosyncratic experience but conceptions as public and general as an axiom of Euclid, expressed in the simplest and commonest words of the language. The basis of communication in the work is intellectual, not emotional, and it is very simple.

That the history of other people, everybody, should go on in the subjective time of Gertrude Stein is justified in that their characters also live in a subjective time which may not be identical with hers but to which her time can be much more readily synchronized than clock time. That is to say the rhythm of a personality can be expressed in a subjective time capable of considerable variation better than in the procrustean objective time of clocks, astronomy, politics, or metronomes. However, it should be said that the subjectivity of Gertrude Stein in this work is very nearly anonymous—it approximates being pure undifferentiated subjectivity, or simply the human mind. She was concerned much later with identity, or biographical human nature, as against the human mind, but here already the stream of thought is scarcely at all qualified by biographical feeling, as it is in Proust for example. This anonymity or "commonplaceness" or impersonality of mind is of course in her case an intellectual thing, even a scientific discipline, but it is parallel to and very like the mentality of the saints whose biographies are lost in their absorption in the present general miracle and the state of grace. Later Gertrude Stein did very handsome things with this resemblance in *Four Saints in Three Acts.*

At any rate, allowing that *The Making of Americans* is written in a subjective time free of a sequence of events, it is, as Gertrude Stein said, written in a continuous present. This does not make history impossible, insofar as "everyone always is repeating the whole of them." Insofar as the whole subjectivity of an individual is there in any moment of its assertion, and since there is virtually no change in that subjectivity from childhood to old age, any formulation or demonstration of the individual character is a complete account of the essential life of that individual and also of the lives of thousands and thousands like him, past, present, and future. In many ways this is, as I said, like the Pentagon building, both appalling and magnificent. Gertrude Stein was accurate in calling it a "monumental" work. As the Escorial is an expression of the nation in its permanent terms, nothingness and glory, and as Versailles expresses the ultimate national equilibrium between concentrated violence and sensuous splendor, so the Pentagon is or was a self-contained labyrinth of simple essential abstractions. That is what *The Making of Americans* is, what any book of Henry James is, what any American is. We are complicated rather than profound, and we have almost no connection with anything, with the earth or the past or with each other. We do try connections and we treat ourselves to debauches of depth, but as ourselves we are complicated and disconnected.

At least there is every reason to think so. But if the reality, the essence of the personality, is disconnected and self-contained, how is it to be expressed directly, that is without simply describing its circumstances and exteriors in the naturalist manner, or even the Proustian manner? Gertrude Stein solves the problem by reproducing its rhythm and telling its final relationships, its ultimate kind. Although the book may seem at first to be an impoverishment of human

56

life, the personal and biographical life, it is rather a heroic insistence that something of the present person does exist in itself, independent of the flux of personal history and the adventitious contents of the consciousness. The isolation of this something is desperately difficult, and its articulation into expression still more so, but I think the book does it. At least it should be recognized that far from lacking a sense of life and personality, as it may seem to at first, the book is based on a closer and really a more loving sense of people than anyone of this century has had, with the possible exception of Sherwood Anderson. Gertrude Stein had, both as herself and as an American, a great gift for tenderness, and tenderness even at the risk of sentimentality was for her a final moral value and a final literary value, even a dogma. Faced with what were, at the end of the last century, the laboratory facts about the composition of personality and the existence of consciousness, she still could not decide that the reality of people was in their events or their impressions, or their looks or their version of the eternal struggle of mythical archetypes or social forces—as most of our writers have done. She was determined to express the essential being, the final mode of existence in people, as a thing in itself and sufficient in itself, independent of their historical and social conditions. This has to be said, because she has been accused often enough and even by her friends, of an inhuman treatment of the human subject. The trouble is that the accusation comes from people who do not understand, as she certainly did, what is properly human and what is not, and that the intelligence—even the scientific intelligence at the time of this book—is a serious human resource, though not more. William James in one way or another may have made this clear to her, but she was, as herself, bound to know it. She honored the human subject enough to treat it as she really saw it, and with all the resources of the human mind she could command.

57

While *The Making of Americans* is a description of American people and properly treats them as disembodied and disconnected, the types described do resume, if not all, most possible human beings, as kinds of subjectivity. It is an interior history of all human beings. Or as she might have said, the inside story of the insides.

Proust, using a subjective time, is still quite different, writing the inside history of the outside or exterior which manifests the various subjectivities of his characters, or at least contains them. This difference is natural to the two nations involved, even on the level of one being a Protestant and the other a Catholic country. The Protestant is essentially disembodied, the Catholic embodied. Thus for Proust subjective time is an element in which objective things are or change—people are giants in time as impressionist objects are in light and atmosphere. But for Gertrude Stein subjective time can be a final reality, a dimension, a plane. It is for her a basis of simplification, not of complication, a plane of reference, not a disintegrating or refractive element.

The Making of Americans happens to coincide more or less with other simplifications at the beginning of the century —Isadora Duncan in the dance, and Satie in music, but more clearly with cubism or the styles that culminated in it, as Gertrude Stein was very much a friend of Picasso at the time and said she was doing in writing what Picasso was doing in painting.

The essential method of cubism is the reduction of the complex natural object to the simplest human spatial abstractions—the straight line, the circle or arc, and the point or dot. A similar thing occurs in early Greek geometric and even in neolithic art, but the more immediate development was out of Cézanne and then Negro sculpture. As Cézanne had reached a very delicate equilibrium between the very complex natural "impressionist" object and human spatial abstractions, the cylinder, cone, and sphere—so Flaubert had

58

in *Madame Bovary* reached a delicate balance between the natural outer context and the inner life of Emma. The cubist movement was a violent destruction of Cézanne's equilibrium, as *The Making of Americans* or even "Melanctha" was a destruction of the equilibrium of Flaubert. As the three-dimensional abstractions of Cézanne were flattened into the two dimensions of cubism, so the biographical dimension of *Madame Bovary* was flattened into the continuous present of *The Making of Americans*. As in straight narrative art the story functions as a plane, the continuous present of interior time was for Gertrude Stein a flat plane of reference, without concern for depth. Solids and depth concerned both Flaubert and Cézanne, but not at this time Gertrude Stein or Picasso.

The change to plane geometry was an advance in simplicity and finality, to absolute elementalism. It contains some interesting motifs for future writing and painting, as for example the use of the letters of the alphabet, the simple juxtaposition of heterogeneous objects, the use of a concrete recognizable object in the midst of abstractions. But the main similarity between cubism and this period of Gertrude Stein's writing is the reduction of outward reality to the last and simplest abstractions of the human mind.

As to its form, *The Making of Americans,* being so intensely of an interior time, must articulate that time as its primary dimension, not the dimensions of external narrative. It cannot rely on the conventional sequences or the habitual interest of external events and received ideas to sustain the expression. All the beginnings and endings, transitions and elaborations and accents, are not conventionally predetermined but have to be constantly determined afresh by the immediate appetite and impulse of the mind deeply engaged with its subject and its medium. After all, the vitality of this impulse is what makes any work exciting to read, even when it uses alien interests as well and the conventional apparatus

59

of events in causal sequence. But in this book the primary creative impulse is there with an extraordinary clarity of presence, constantly making its decisions, word by word, doing it all, taking nothing for granted.

Gertrude Stein said the business of the artist is to be exciting. Exactly that, and no amount of secondary virtues like intelligence and moral rectitude and technical ingenuity can replace it. Everybody knows this, but actually very few artists are alive enough to have this inner vitality command the rest. That is where genius comes in. Artists of talent usually try to replace being exciting with being excited, a difference Gertrude Stein put as the distinction between saints and hysterics in artists, as the difference between being alive and being lively. At any rate, this vitality of the writer, as against the given interest of the subject matter, is conveyed mostly as it creates or conducts the form. It is conveyed also as it possesses its own vision of the subject matter, but the particular vision is again embodied in the form.

The form of *The Making of Americans* being temporal, the subject matter is seen and presented as a process in time. As I said the character of Melanctha was "played," so the subject matter of this book, whether characters, types, ideas, a feeling or a scene, is all in a way "played." The time is of course articulated by rhythm, but also in units which are the paragraphs. These are conceived not merely as a rhetorical problem but, something like a passage in music, as the registration of a space of time, as a habitable and operable and continuous present. Naturally any one paragraph can be short or long, depending on the time it takes for the impulse of the writer to reach the culmination or saturation of what it has to do with the subject matter. Since the business of Gertrude Stein in this work is not remarking things and their qualities and sequences only but presenting them in time, it is often a very long business. She has to dwell not

60

so much on the subject as with it. The paragraph is made complete, as any natural activity is made complete, by satisfaction, or having enough. This sense of adequacy, of fullness, of everything being accounted for, depends, as in music that is music and not musicology, not on simply exhausting the subject but on a balance of relationships and a rhythm of succession within the paragraph—something like the rhetorical balance and the completion of the rhyme scheme in a stanza of poetry. When the full organic balance is reached, that is that, until the next time. The going on to the next time and the next led Gertrude Stein to compositions by series and lists and the like—corresponding for interior time to the episodic treatment of exterior events. This construction, which became one of her favorites and which I shall discuss more fully later, is already present in *The Making of Americans*, where each paragraph is made to be a complete interior event.

Within the paragraph the relations of ideas, the syntactical relations, the succession of sentences, are made to move and cohere and balance, to have a conduct and a phrasing that reproduce the specific pressure or dynamic balance of the experienced subject matter, whether it be a person, a type, an idea, a feeling, or even an event. This can be seen in the following presentation of an event from the inside.

This one, and the one I am now beginning describing is Martha Hersland and this is a little story of the acting in her of her being in her very young living, this one was a very little one then and she was running and she was in the street and it was a muddy one and she had an umbrella that she was dragging and she was crying. "I will throw the umbrella in the mud," she was saying, she was very little then, she was just beginning her schooling, "I will throw the umbrella in the mud," she said and no one was near her and she was dragging the umbrella and bitterness possessed her, "I

61

will throw the umbrella in the mud," she was saying and nobody heard her, the others had run ahead to get home and they had left her, "I will throw the umbrella in the mud," and there was desperate anger in her; "I have throwed the umbrella in the mud," burst from her, she had thrown the umbrella in the mud and that was the end of it all in her. She had thrown the umbrella in the mud and no one heard her as it burst from her, "I have throwed the umbrella in the mud," it was the end of all that to her.[26]

Here the paragraph is synchronized with the rise and exhaustion of the rage of the little girl, but there is the same sort of progressive realization and coming to have enough when the subject is an entirely different thing, an idea or whatever.

Disillusionment in living is the finding out nobody agrees with you not those that are and were fighting with you. Disillusionment in living is the finding out nobody agrees with you not those that are fighting for you. Complete disillusionment is when you realise that no one can for they can't change. The amount they agree is important to you until the amount they do not agree with you is completely realised by you. Then you say you will write for yourself and strangers, you will be for yourself and strangers and this then makes an old man or an old woman of you.[27]

. . . . . .

When he was not at all a very young one sometimes he was with one. Sometimes he was with more than one. Sometimes he was with two sometimes he was with more than two. Sometimes he was with three. Sometimes he was with more than three. Sometimes he was with four. Sometimes he

26. *The Making of Americans* (Harcourt, Brace, 1934), p. 232.
27. *Ibid.*, p. 282.

62

*was with more than four. Sometimes he was with five. Some-
times he was with more than five.*[28]

. . . . . .

*Old ones come to be dead. Any one coming to be an old
enough one comes to be a dead one. Old ones come to be
dead ones. Any one not coming to be a dead one before
coming to be an old one comes to be an old one and comes
then to be a dead one as any old one comes to be a dead
one.*[29]

The paragraph often gets its independent completion
from its being a new beginning in the endless vital process
of "beginning again and again" by keeping very steadily to
its own time and its own balance, without support from suggestions or assumption outside itself. It began to be very
much a thing existing in itself, and while it was an exact
duplicate or re-creation of an experienced reality, it was
so highly organized in the terms of its own abstractions that
its quality of being true, true to life as everyone and science
vaguely know it, and *recognizably* so, grew less and less important. The break with naturalism and recognizability came
in the course of the next work, "A Long Gay Book," but the
crisis is being prepared in *The Making of Americans.*

Gertrude Stein describes the abandonment of the book
as a natural consequence of having realized that after all she
could very easily have described all she knew about all con-
ceivable kinds of people, and she did know a great deal.
One difficulty she mentions had been the expression, as a
present thing, of knowledge which had been acquired piece-
meal over a long time and with endless effort. While she had
pretty well succeeded in expressing what she knew about
anyone or any type in a single resumptive paragraph, and

28. *Ibid.,* p. 376.
29. *Ibid.,* p. 413.

while all the knowledge was present to her in writing, it was after all knowledge with a history, it brought her fully prepared to the subject which was thereby perfectly familiar, and if familiar was thereby not existing purely in the present. "So then I said I would begin again. I would not know what I knew about everything what I knew about anything. . . . And so it was necessary to let come what would happen to come . . ."[30]

This is an important difference, not only to literature. As Gertrude Stein said, quoting Lord Grey, in entering a war nations are prepared to fight not the coming war but the previous war.[31] Preparation then is at odds with that which makes the present present, that is with what is new. Anyone can see how this is a situation obtaining generally, in war, in the personal life, in philosophy, in business, in anything. As the artist is the one who, according to Gertrude Stein, is the most sensitive exponent of his contemporaneity, that is the one who must express the essential newness of what is there, of what happens to come, he is the one who must above all be prepared for the unexpected. He can only be prepared to be at a loss except for his medium and his force of attention. This is the sort of thing Gide meant by *disponibilité*, and was in the vogue for primitivism, for the *naïf*, and the general simplification of means.

Seriously done, the change meant giving up science, for science is description and prediction in terms of the already familiar. And so it meant giving up intelligibility in the familiar terms of science and history. As philosophy, as Gertrude Stein had learned at Radcliffe, comes after the descriptions of science, and as religion comes before them, the nearest mental attitudes to this art of the new present, the unique present, are precisely the philosophical and the religious. Or, more availably, the childlike. With Gertrude

30. *Lectures in America*, p. 158.
31. *Composition as Explanation*, p. 6.
64

Stein the new attitude had to involve all at once the dialectic, a sense of the miraculous, and the playful. This is contained in a little passage of the second portrait of Picasso:

> *Miracles play.*
> *Play fairly.*
> *Play fairly well.*[32]

But the beginning of all this belongs to the next chapter. *The Making of Americans* was left behind, by Gertrude Stein. It contained too much 19th century science and history, though it also contained the beginnings of 20th century American writing. These beginnings were stylistic, but more essentially in the creation of a really independent time continuum in the written thing.

History aside, *The Making of Americans* has the essential quality of a masterpiece, the continuous presence of active mind applied to something alive.

32. *Portraits and Prayers*, p. 25.

3. Insides and Outsides

As the problem of time and narrative is always there in literature, to be solved another way each time, so is the problem of space and physical description. Or, to use the plainer terminology of Gertrude Stein, there is the outside to be described as well as the inside. The question of the outside is especially acute for American writers because, as she said, Americans are disembodied. We have neither the same attachment to the land nor the same use of the senses as the English, who created the language and the greater part of its literary tradition.

For the English the landscape is a reasonably small habitable thing melting and rolling and growing and fading with the seasons, and any blooming of a wild flower or falling of rain, any little incident of natural process, is a perfectly full and sufficient reality. English poetry and the English novel are naturally full of it, full of a space made of weather and the happy or melancholy welter of natural process. But space for us is no such thing. It is mainly distance for us, and so inclined to be empty and flat. In the past it has offered us temporary places and material but we do not settle into it except as distance when we move. This reduces us to having to make a special program of describing American things, a regional, political, or philosophical program, or to describing foreign things. Space is for us an exotic, even romantic thing and objects in it cannot have for us a simple literal meaning,

66

as given presences. They have to have a symbolic meaning or a romantic value. Hawthorne, Melville, Emily Dickinson, Henry James, Hart Crane, T. S. Eliot, and especially the imagists, all have to convert physical objects into something else before they can be there in the writing. In James they turn out to be as large and principled and incorporeal as his human characters. The conversation of his houses speaking in the character of their architectural styles is an extreme instance.

The logic of her work brought Gertrude Stein rather abruptly against this problem of the physical world. *Three Lives,* it is true, had treated the physical world very expertly, but rather as an accompaniment to character, not as a radically different reality. But *The Making of Americans* had suppressed the physical world almost entirely, in order to disengage the simple persistence of the character in time. That project of describing all possible kinds of people "as they are to themselves inside them" was all but completely done, in 1908. But very evidently the external and incidental relationships or manifestations of the inner existence remained to be done, and part of the project of the next work, "A Long Gay Book," begun in 1909, was the description of all possible kinds of pairs or "twos" of people, and threes and fours, and on to crowds. At the same time the "flavor" of the characters, their specific variation from the major type, was to be presented in their "little ways" of sitting or leaning or disposing of their time or saying anything and so on. This project, which looked promising enough and was successful enough so far as it was taken in "A Long Gay Book," ran into various difficulties and was, in that form, abandoned.

The main difficulty was that the presentation of two or more human interiors together naturally tends to be dramatic —which would mean a return to the method of "Melanctha" or even to plots and intrigues, events, which would make the character at any given time relative to his action, so sunk in particulars that his meaning as a type or even as an existence in himself would be obscured. Even his "little ways" would become part of the quality of the scenes or events, not distinctly a full expression or manifestation of character, still less what Gertrude Stein was beginning to make of them, a sufficient reality in themselves.[1]

If the dramatic order was false to the purpose, then a simple list, a simple juxtaposition of typical instances, or the grouping of an arbitrary number of instances under a category was the simple and natural solution. Gertrude Stein was never afraid of a simple solution. Some of the titles of this period—"A Man," "Five or Six Men," "Two," "Five," "Four Dishonest Ones," etc.—are very pleased with it, and so in particular is the story "Many Many Women." It is a lovely story, I think, but it does rest on a knowledge and a method the conquest of which was done and more exciting in *The Making of Americans*.[2] Gertrude Stein said of herself that she had a great deal of inertia, and she did sometimes stay on with her own methods for the pleasure they could still give her, but at this time the method was going to have to change —because she was beginning to feel that her own knowledge of people was getting in her way, between her and immediate experience. "Because as my life was my life inside me but I

1. For example, in "A Long Gay Book," *Matisse Picasso and Gertrude Stein* (Plain Edition, 1933), p. 71: "Pulling and going is regularly sounding and answering is intermittently continuing. Running and disappearing and gesticulating and waiting is happening."
2. Gertrude Stein later said (*Lectures in America*, p. 148) that "Many Many Women" and some other shorter works were meant to "illustrate" the chief book, "A Long Gay Book," so it is to some extent a secondary work. There may be some use in making a canon of the principle and secondary works of Gertrude Stein, but I do not know enough to attempt it. Whatever the "place" of "Many Many Women," Miss Toklas says that Gertrude Stein thoroughly enjoyed herself writing it, and it shows.

was realizing beginning realizing that everything described would not do any more than tell all I knew about anything . . . since after all I did know all I knew about anything.

"So then I said I would begin again. I would not know what I knew about everything what I knew about anything." [3]

This need for a *dépouillement* or stripping was not rare with Gertrude Stein and she knew it was frequent with Picasso. It is also, of course, a fairly usual impulse with saints, and it is remarkable how closely connected with religious interests and disciplines the general "primitive" movement of the period was—Apollinaire, Jacob, Satie, Rousseau. Whether it is worth saying or not, one may say it was in the air, it was contemporary. It was certainly connected with a general contraction of the historical sense, so that, as Gertrude Stein said, civilization did not seem very old,[4] and all historical styles from the paleolithic on became all but contemporary. Sufficiently so to undermine the historical romanticism of the 19th century, its intoxication with great distances in time as well as in space. So that the grandeur of universal knowledge and cosmic significance was less exciting than the intensity of immediate particular knowledge. Or what William James had been preaching long before as "pure" experience.

All that being in the air, what precipitated the change for Gertrude Stein was a trip to Granada in 1911. She suddenly

3. *Lectures in America,* p. 158.
4. *Ibid.,* pp. 151–153.
Also in *Lucy Church Amiably* (Plain Edition, 1930), p. 192, there is the sentence: "If it surprises him that there are only sixty generations between him and Jesus Christ why does it surprise him?"
Among the American disconnections is certainly a disengagement from historical continuity, and this allowed Gertrude Stein to be naturally abreast of the movement in painting at least, in Paris before the first World War. What she did with history in literature I shall discuss in later chapters.

rediscovered the visible world. She had been to Spain before, to Granada, she had known Picasso for some time, and she had been looking at paintings intently for a very long while, but this visit was decisive because of the question in her mind about existence as both immediate and final, and because of the nature of the landscape of Spain, which is eminently both immediate and final.

It does not change and melt and grow like an English landscape nor can it be reduced to distances like an American landscape. After all, Spain is a peninsula and one soon runs out of all except perhaps vertical distances. The landscape and the things in or on it are absolutely and fully there. They make a challenge to man, to be, as absolutely, as unchangeably, as they are. Man has to counter the landscape with an equivalent reality. Which is what not only the *Quijote* but also the saints of Greco, the arabesques of the Alhambra, the *Cid*, the Spanish mystics, the inventions of Picasso, the rhetoric of Seneca, and the rituals of bullfighting are all about. More indulgent landscapes, like those of France and England, lead to a different art and mentality, against which all Spanish things look excessive and overdone.

Physical presence, corporeal presence, is a finality in Spain and indeed the final test of any reality, so that the religion and the literature and the thinking are all dense with images. Even the words of the Spanish language are *things*, with a solidity, a distinctness, an intractable finality of their own. They are the best possible words, now that Latin is over, to go into bronze lettering, as happens all over Madrid. They have nothing of the elasticity of English words, nor are they capable of nuance and reserve and inflection like French. Whether it comes plain or fancy, Spanish is a stone or metal language.

The primacy of physical presence is such in Spain that any constructed thing, a painting or a poem or a statue or whatever, not only is not obliged to but simply cannot depend on

70

its resemblance to other physical things for its reality. It has to stand by the force of its own immediate and proper qualities. To the extent that when Spanish art goes realistic it is so completely real that it destroys all memory of an original, as a wax dummy creates its own obsessive presence and does not remind you of anything. It is on this same basis, moreover, that the Spanish, like nobody else, take surrealism in their stride. But the Moorish arabesque and the Byzantine were at home in Spain, and the violent distortions of the baroque were quite possible and natural, in painting, architecture, and literature. Góngora is a good example of it in literature, but more recently the work of Lorca and the *greguerías* of Ramón Gomez de la Serna show the constancy of a method based on simple and unquestionable physical presence. The greguerías are quite like the "Spanish" period of Gertrude Stein, like *Tender Buttons,* but there is no question of influence; [5] both derive directly from the landscape of Spain.

This confrontation with the simple final presence of landscape must have been very exciting to Gertrude Stein, as she then possessed an interior time reduced to a simple final present. The problem of relating the two in writing must have been irresistible, especially as she had seen two striking solutions in other arts—Spanish dancing and bullfighting [6]

5. There is no question of influence either between Gertrude Stein and Max Jacob, though they were friends and though there are similarities enough between *Le Cornet à Dés* and some of Gertrude Stein's work. She did not read his work until she was well along in her new style and beyond influence. But she naturally liked it when she did read it. They were both influenced in some degree by the painting of Picasso, but rather as a corroboration than as a model.

6. The Spanish dance is directly imitated in "Susie Asado" and "Preciosilla." Indirectly it governs much of the composition of "In the Grass" and "A Sweet Tail." The bullfight is described at about the beginning of the change of styles in "A Long Gay Book." However, this is all more important for the plays and operas that come later than for *Tender Buttons.*

71

—where the greatest possible pressure of immediate spiritual meaning is put upon the physical, where the minutest physical differences make all the difference. Naturally she could not properly have anything to do with the ritualistic or with the legendary meanings of Spanish art, or with its tragic meanings; instead she went to the source of all that, the final and fatal existence of an inner and an outer world in the immediate present. The Spanish present—shown well enough by the lack of any serious historical sense and the lack of any prudence about the future in the French or English manner —was very like her own present [7] though she had not reached it by way of spatial existence. Rather she had come to spatial existence of necessity, through her extreme reduction of time. Still, she took to the Spanish situation readily, and she believed it was enough like an American way of existing in time, that there was for this and many other reasons a natural sympathy between Americans and Spaniards.

Now, in 1951, when so much has happened, the situation between America and Spain may be superseded or obscured by a common orientalism, I do not know. But even if the influence of Spain was for Gertrude Stein and many others a passing exoticism and, in her case, coincided with a spell of romanticism, it was still the nearest thing abroad to an American sense of space, the contrariety of an inner life to space. [8]

7. Cf. *Everybody's Autobiography*, p. 27: ". . . as Picasso says he likes Dali because Dali, like himself, and that is Spanish bases everything on his own ignorance." In 1911 Gertrude Stein was basing herself on a deliberate ignorance ("I would not know what I knew"), for the sake of extricating an immediate reality. The Spanish ignorance, or virginity, or nudity before the present, is essential and, since Seneca at least, very well known. The classic account of it is in Angel Ganivet's *Idearium Español*.

8. Cf. *Everybody's Autobiography*, p. 312: ". . . the Spaniards who naturally always think of space as being filled—well filled with emptiness and suspicion." This perfectly describes the space in Henry James, and for that matter in Hawthorne. But it

Native or not, her commitment to the final being of the mind and to the final being of the physical world made her writing less and less historical, or scientific, or moral—that is, less relational, and more and more metaphysical or religious. William James remarked that any total and final attitude toward life could as well be called a religion, and in that sense the work of Gertrude Stein is religious, it is forever concerned with finalities.

The great welter of what seem to be particularities and trivialities in *Tender Buttons* comes from a "religious" attitude toward everything as simple existence.[9] She said the change at this time was from feeling that everything was simply alike to feeling that everything was simply different, and that "simply different" was the constant intention of these works.[10] In *The Making of Americans* her love of any resemblance and her scientific habit of formulating types had given the characters much of their meaning as being recognizable and classifiable, as standing for millions like them. Their individual differences or mixtures had been sub-

should be said that the Spanish can live with space as a finality and so can paint, whereas we on the whole do not. Probably because our instinct is to consume space or destroy it by movement.

9. It is rather like the sacristy of the Cartuja at Granada, which is a marvel but can scarcely be endured without a very simple poetic or religious enthusiasm for sheer stuff. However, Gertrude Stein was not influenced either by the Cartuja or by the Alhambra but by the landscape around them. The landscape calls for concentration and festivity, for altars and fountains, for enclosures and openings and what comes is the Cartuja, the Alhambra, Lorca, and *Tender Buttons*.

10. *Composition as Explanation*, p. 21. Cf. also *Tender Buttons* (Claire Marie, 1914), p. 63: "Act so that there is no use in a center." That is as essential an expression as one is likely to find anywhere of the rejection of classicism by romanticism. Classicism bases itself throughout on the sense of a center. When, later, Gertrude Stein began to work with the notion of "a simple center and a continuous design"—or of "distribution and equilibration" —she had come back to classicism.

ordinated to the type, seen as variations of or from it. But by rejecting her knowledge of types, Gertrude Stein was faced with each experience as a unique thing, with even its importance unprejudiced, as simply different. It is logical enough that anything is the same as something else by some category or other, but it is also unique, by being both the only thing in its space at the time and the only thing before the mind if the mind attends to it.

This direct sense of things as unique and unclassified is of course very exciting to the person possessed of the sense, it gives an early freshness and glamor to experience, as if it were constantly a new or renewed world, just begun or begun again; but the problem of expressing or reproducing the experience, beyond simple exclamation, is enormous. Gertrude Stein called it romanticism and said that of course it would be at first very inarticulate. The work of this period is full of exclamation like romantic poetry but it gradually developed a highly efficient articulation.

Gertrude Stein as usual began at the beginning, with the question of how anything is put together, of how anyone puts something together, whether it be a day or a wedding cake or a poem or a syllogism or buttons in a box. And how does one really put the data of experience together to make a sense? Things are together well enough by being next to each other and very well if inside something, whether a moment of consciousness, a space, or an action. But how does one get together with anything? The simplest way is by counting it, and Gertrude Stein never did give up counting. But almost as simple a way is to name it—love, apple, mantel-piece, or whatever—and so relate it to vocabulary, or to a category like passion, fruit, or furniture, or to its habitual situation in a story if there is one, all of this belonging not to the original perceived thing but to us, to the human interior. Thus the perceived thing is accounted for, organized, possessed. It is converted into a substantive, a settled thing,

74

quite as if it had been counted. But the original experience may have been nothing of the kind. The mantelpiece may have been seen as a difficult or obliging level, as a whole adventure in following marble veining, as the sustaining of an elbow or bric-a-brac. So that the name "mantelpiece" does not get one together with anything but a memory of something else. Any name, unless it is put into a situation which shocks it into meaning, gradually does not have any vividness or convey any actuality of experience, and much of the effort in *Tender Buttons* is to replace or to shock the name of anything in order to restore the sense of immediate unprepared experience.

For example, this description called "A Method of a Cloak":

A single climb to a line, a straight exchange to a cane, a desperate adventure and courage and a clock, all this which is a system, which has feeling, which has resignation and success, all makes an attractive black silver.[11]

What is being described here is of course not what everyone knows about cloaks or expects of them generally but what was actually experienced in looking directly at one once, the style of the lines and folds felt as a distinct impression—their dash and regularity at once. In this poem at least one can reconstruct closely enough what the original experience was like. The "clock" may be a metaphor for regularity of interval in the folds, but otherwise the ordinary meaning of each word is enough to re-create the experience about as sharply as any experience of the kind can be re-created in words.

There are many attempts to render the exact impression of color in terms of action, of sound in terms of color and emotion, of shape in terms of action and character.

11. *Tender Buttons*, pp. 13–14.

Go red go red, laugh white.[12]

A tiny violent noise is a yellow happy thing. A yellow happy thing is a gentle little tinkle that goes in all the way it has everything to say. It is not what there was when it was not where it is. It is all that it is when it is all that there is.[13]

A CUTLET
A blind agitation is manly and uttermost.[14]

Though all this is composed from "private" impressions, the impressions are here conveyed clearly enough. Though the impression of "yellow" for example varies endlessly in other contexts, it is quite clear what the exact impression was in this case—that is, not so mellow as the usual "golden," and giddier. One can also convert "that goes in all the way, it has everything to say" into the commonplace descriptions of such sounds: "penetrating, garrulous"; but such conversions and explanations do not make it more vivid. All they do is to let one recognize it as one's own experience more vividly and sharply seen. But most of the work of this period is not recognizable in that way, at least not to me. For example:

COLD CLIMATE
A season in yellow sold extra strings makes lying places.[15]

In that poem I do not in the least recognize the subject matter, nor do I think there is any possibility for anyone who has not spent a good deal of time in the contemplation of fringe and the like to recognize it even in a general way. One may, with a little ingenuity, invent a specific or general meaning to fit the words—as, "a natural duration of attention

12. *Ibid.*, p. 27.
13. "A Long Gay Book," p. 82.
14. *Tender Buttons*, p. 21.
15. *Ibid.*, p. 22.

76

to some decorative yellow fancy strings comes down to recognition of relaxed horizontals," or, "living a while in bright mercenary luxurious attachments results in abject objectivity." It would be quite possible to go through all the work of this period and get a complete set of such commonplace glosses. It is amusing to invent them and the result may have a certain charm. But it is perfectly idle. Such a procedure puts the original in the position of being a riddle, a rhetorical complication of something rather unremarkable in itself. It would be rather like an exhibition of the original table tops, guitars, pipes, and people which were the subject matter of cubist paintings. The original subject matter is or was of importance to the painter as a source of sensations, relations, ideas even, but it is not after all the beholder's business. The beholder's business is the picture in front of him, which is a new reality and something else, which does not add up to the nominal subject matter. But can the subject matter of writing be treated in the same way, to be lost in or superseded by the resultant work? And if it can be, should it?

This is still, by midcentury, a matter of dispute, and one has to go into it a little. If the subject matter is of no importance to the beholder of a picture or the reader of a literary work, is there any reason for the subject matter to have been there in the first place? That is one question or more, and another is, what is the beholder or the reader to make of the finished product if he cannot measure it against a recognizable subject matter?

The answer to the first question is that subject matter is a necessity to the artist. The interior life by itself, to itself, is extremely vacant and indefinite, if it exists at all, except potentially. As subject matter, it can be isolated from all but its most primitive relations, as in *The Making of Americans,* but it is always about the same, always persisting in its same basic attitude and relations. It has nothing, as Gertrude Stein said, to make it "connectedly different," [16] at least to itself. Even when it relates itself to ideas or to things it does not vary much, and goes through a very limited number of simple operations. But the thing, the moment, created by the duration of the relationship, whether an experience or a creation, can be enormously varied and interesting. In short, objective material, perception, is not only a condition of variety and range of quality but the basis of excitement and even, strictly, of consciousness. Without an object the mind simply goes blank and to sleep. An art without subject matter is really not possible. Highly abstract and nonrepresentational paintings, for example, when there is no trace of naturalistic subject matter, have simply taken spatial relations and color relations, whether or not geometrized and schematized, as their subject matter, and the trouble there is that the art tends to be extremely narrow if intense and "pure." It is very liable to mechanical formula and decorativism, since the range of what the mind can do with nothing more than prefabricated abstractions like geometry and the spectrum is not very great, for either the artist or the beholder. Abstraction as the process of abstracting compositional elements directly out of the complex reality before us is one thing, but the manipulation of simple conventions on their own is another thing and academic.

A remark about Picabia by Gertrude Stein will help here:

Picabia had conceived and is struggling with the problem that a line should have the vibration of a musical sound and that this vibration should be the result of conceiving the human form and the human face in so tenuous a fashion that it would induce such vibration in the line forming it. . . .

The surréalistes taking the manner for the matter as is the way with the vulgarisers, accept the line as having become vibrant and as therefore able in itself to inspire them to

16. *Composition as Explanation*, p. 23.
78

higher flights. He who is going to be the creator of the vibrant line knows that it is not yet created and if it were it would not exist by itself, it would be dependent upon the emotion of the object which compels the vibration.[17]

That is the predicament of the artist and the writer alike, certainly and very consciously of Gertrude Stein; they are perfectly dependent on subject matter. But evidently they are artists, and their initial vision of the subject matter is not the standard or average practical vision of their contemporaries, and they are further governed by the impulse to make something of it, so that what may still be recognizable in the result is only an incident or a circumstance. It may or may not be the business of criticism to reduce the work of art to its incidents and all its elements and reassemble it again to show how it was done in the first place, but this mechanistic understanding of the process should be kept distinct from the appreciation and enjoyment of the result. It is this last that is really our business, and the question now.

The sense of the special and immediate existence of a literary work more or less in itself is most familiar to us perhaps in poetry. There is in the first place the metric and the rhyme scheme, the repetitions of sound and rhythmic units and words, which do not belong to anything but the poem and help to mark its existence off from the rest of reality, to isolate it.[18] Feelings, sensations, ideas, all the material which

17. *The Autobiography of Alice B. Toklas*, p. 174.
18. This is one reason Gertrude Stein used elementary metrics and rhyme in prose as well as poetry. Other devices for insisting on the reality of the work are her use of initials, as G.M.P., of Roman numerals after names, as with kings, of mistakes and corrections in the midst of sentences, and of course the "cryptogram":

	stand	take	to	taking
	we	you	throw	our

79

has its origin in the other reality, in history, but which is brought into the poem, takes on a quite new weight, bearing, coloration, relationships, in short it changes its meaning radically in order to compose a new and unique meaning, which is the poem. All that is commonplace enough, and everyone is aware that words and ideas have a reality distinct from experience, that rhetoric and grammar do not correspond to thinking as it goes on in anybody's head. We know that literature is a different reality from life, and that it is differently organized. The confusion comes from the materials that are common to both art and life.

Naturally any word at all contains to start with an abstraction from many experiences in life, and each word in isolation does convey a generality which is used in life, in thinking and in conversation about particular complexes of experience. Any word if it is a traditional word is bound to convey its generality.[19] In this way they are like numbers, like 1, 2, 3, which inevitably convey the generality of unity or of duality or of triads, no matter what particular things you may be counting. Words by themselves have much the same finality and simple solid meaning as numbers. One may or may not feel the necessity for imaginary words as one may or may not feel the necessity for imaginary numbers. In any case our question is not about words in isolation but about words in composition. Any words in any order inevitably create a situation, and it is the situations created by words in composition that may or may not be recognizable, as habitual situations in thinking and experience. Or rather as situations habitually imposed on thinking and experience, since the situations of grammatical syntax, the assumption of a substantive and the attachment of a predicate to it and the addition of qualifications to either or both, are all perfectly conventional and arbitrary. But they constitute a human in-

19. Cf. *Lectures in America*, p. 230: "It is extraordinary how it is impossible that a vocabulary does not make sense."

80

strument for making a human sense of life and experience, they are already rudimentary art forms. Life makes "sense" insofar as it is reducible to art forms of some kind, simple or complicated. One may say that anything whatever will make a certain amount of sense if put into grammatical syntax; as one follows the development of relationships and enjoys the nouns in listening to double talk. In short, the simple formal relationships, the verbal elements in a literary work, constitute in themselves an independent reality and a sense. That much is automatically given. To be interesting the work has to have a fuller and further sense, and that has to come from life. It can be a number of things.

One further sense is in keeping between the things mentioned in the work more or less the same relationships as exist between them in everyone's generalized and conventionalized memory of such things: as roses are red and relate to love, beauty, and mortality. That is, one does not, in such writing, describe the actual imperfect white rose in the disaffected cheese glass on one's table or on the underside of its bush as *the* rose. Another sense is of course the allegorical or symbolical sense, in which the relationships are reproductions of the relationships in specific knowledge outside the work, as in Dante, or Spenser, or T. S. Eliot, or Milton often enough. But the relations of outside knowledge, whether general or particular, are realized within the poem and are converted to concrete relations within the poem. That is, when one is reading a poem involving roses one is knowing the roses of the poem, at a certain place in the line, not other roses or roses in general, though the vague memory of these may color and enrich the immediate literary roses; and one reads Dante as the complexities and involutions of the *Commedia*, not as the complexities and involutions of cosmology, astronomy, and Florentine politics.

The phrase of Milton, "blind mouths," may be, for the historical critic, about the voracity of the clergy, and mean

81

that Milton didn't like it, but for the reader with his mind on the text of "Lycidas" the voracity of the clergy and Milton's feeling about it are both pretexts or ingredients for the creation of this new and wonderful thing: blind mouths.[20] For the reader, Milton and the clergy, if they get into it at all, get their meaning from the phrase, not the other way round. The phrase exists in itself, with its own heavy, strained, violent character, its own beauty if you like, and it is only our weakness and our prosaic curiosity that makes us want to know the reason and the occasion for the phrase, where its character comes from. It domesticates the phrase, puts it in a cage, back in the 17th century context, so that we no longer have to face it directly. The clergy and Milton's indignation about it were, however, quite necessary to give the phrase its character, its "sense," beyond the simple vocabulary senses of "blind" and "mouths" and the syntactical sense of noun and adjective.

For the writer another source of such further sense is the conversion of previously inarticulate knowledge, or unprejudiced and primitive experience, into the senses of literary composition. This is, of course, the attempt of *Tender Buttons*. Insofar as the relations do not as yet exist for the reader either in general or specific knowledge, the work is dependent on the formal resources of writing to create a thing with a sense as distinct and full as a work using prefabricated senses to sustain its sense. These resources should not be underestimated.

There is of course the verbal rhythm, the texture and behavior of consonants and vowels, all of which do register or convey a more vital thing, "style." Style is the whole behavior of the artist's mind conducting the composition, choosing, insisting, interrupting, reverting, and so on. It is the

20. Cf. the first sentence of *An Acquaintance with Description* (Seizin Press, 1928): "Mouths and Wood." Here we simply do not know the pretext.

essence, the proper and perfectly appreciable vitality of any work, and it may be conveyed in all the dimensions of the work—from the choice and disposition of the subject matter down to the punctuation. It is conveyed to an astonishing degree even when one does not recognize the subject matter, even when the work is in a foreign language one does not fully understand. Or when, as in some fragments of Sappho, only two or three words are left of a poem. In music, and by now in painting, we are quite accustomed to attending to the events and movements and impulses of the style to the exclusion of other interests. We are even more accustomed, in life, to catching the whole character of a person from a single intonation, a single turn of the head or hand. We are not so accustomed to doing this in reading literature, though it can be and is done. Gertrude Stein can be and is often read for the sheer pleasure of the style so far as it is conveyed by the sound and look of the words. But in literature the basic means are not essentially sensory—as with the sound of music or the color and line of painting; words are primarily intellectual, conceptual. Each one embodies or presents its general idea, and these general ideas should be the major compositional means of any literary work. Philosophically as well as artistically speaking, ideas are compositional means. We know it from Plato's philosophical mimes and we know it from Pope and we know it from propaganda, but we do forget it. We have trouble not thinking that the formulated or crystallized ideas within the work or deducible from the work are the meaning and measure of the work itself.

If the words as ideas in a work are not arranged according to the conventions of logic or the habitual groupings of ideas in life, one can most easily approach them like a circus or a miracle or the tricks of a magician. One should be as intellectually direct and ready as a child or a saint, with a flair for the impossible, for coincidences and collisions, for puns, paradoxes, slapstick, and the outrageous. *Tender Buttons* and a great deal of the work of Gertrude Stein can quite fairly be taken as a sort of Wonderland or Luna Park for anybody who is not too busy. Or, if you are willing to look at the 20th century as it is, forgetting what it should be or how it came to be like that or where it is leading, it is quite like *Tender Buttons*. That much, I should say, is immediately appreciable in *Tender Buttons*, and what more does one really want?

Because this style that maintains constantly the marvelous and the unexpected, the arbitrary and the absurd, quite aside from its likeness to the century, is an expression of as serious a philosophical position and as valid and heroic a way of life as any, which is that man can and must constantly and, in the last analysis, arbitrarily, choose for himself and be on his own. If he looks to see what he remembers, to verify his preconceptions and what he has been told, if he looks in order to be right and useful and necessary, that is one thing, but if he looks to see what he does not already know or what is there now and what he can make of it, he is alive. The philosophy is radically one of freedom within a fairly strict empiricism. The reader can read the work in the light of the philosophical implications in the large, or he can ignore them. Abstracting and formulating such implications may be the business of the critic if he chooses, but they are properly qualities of a work, not its thesis.

All the same I think one has to like freedom in order to like Gertrude Stein's work at all. One has to want a work to be itself, on its own, and not on the tolerance or justification of philosophy, history, journalism, economics, or whatever, even aesthetics. As one presumably wants to be, oneself. One has to want a work to find its own spontaneous logic and form its ideas on the way rather than follow out a preconception. Gertrude Stein can be thought of as a thoroughly civilized woman operating in Indian territory with the extreme wakefulness and adroitness required by such a situation. She did love the stories of missionaries and explorers, and *Robinson Crusoe* was one of her favorite books. As more and more people go over the same ground, her work will seem more natural, as the work of the romantic poets seems natural to us now because several generations have been over and over that ground. In their time they seemed completely unreal. But now, what gives a distinct quality and a sense not only to the early 19th century but to whole territories of human experience is the character of Byron's verse, or of Keats', or of Shelley's, or of the prose of Chateaubriand. The byronic and the keatsian are perfectly precise terms, defining as constant a reality as for example the "napoleonic." And it is perfectly possible that the first half of this century, in which everything has been wildly disconnected and at the same time almost anything is made to connect with anything else, may find its most exact meaning in the word "steinesque." [21]

As for the way *Tender Buttons* was written, its subject matter and the techniques used on it for its conversion into the work as it stands, I know very little about it. Still, something is known, and Gertrude Stein was informative about it. In the first place, the subject matter of *Tender Buttons*— objects, food, rooms—was chosen for a definite reason. It corresponds to the "still life," the familiar objects on a table top, that were used as basic subject matter by the cubists.[22]

21. In the epilogue to her book on Picasso she explains how his painting is like the 20th century: ". . . it is a time when everything cracks, where everything is destroyed, everything isolates itself, it is a more splendid thing than a period where everything follows itself." *Picasso* (B. T. Batsford, 1938), p. 49. She was very conscious of being the one to create the composition of her time in writing.

22. Cf. *The Autobiography of Alice B. Toklas*, p. 99: ". . . the difficulty that the artist feels and which sends him to painting still lifes, that after all the human being essentially is not paintable. . . . No, she stayed with her task [describing people], although after the return to Paris she described objects, she described rooms

As the created reality and not the original reality had to be everything in the cubist picture, the original reality had to be as simple and familiar as possible, to contain nothing but a visual interest and even that visual interest as unprejudiced as possible by tradition. The miracle had to take place where everyone could see it and where it would be least expected. Or, if one likes, a new world had to be discovered or created here and now, under one's nose. Gertrude Stein, thoroughly a realist, and now completely interested in the finality of anything existing in space, naturally took as her subject matter the most familiar objects in what was to her as a woman the most familiar place, the household. If the things most nullified by habit could be brought alive by a new vision and a new method, something of radical importance would be done, not only in art but for living. A dull or latent vision in the general public could perhaps be brought into full consciousness, as any seriously new artistic or literary vision wakens something of the same vision in the public and makes more of the general life. There was a good deal of the fuss of a secret society about the early cubists, but cubism has since been so endlessly vulgarized in architecture, interior decorating, advertising layouts, and so on that it has been responsible for a serious revolution in vision; and while Gertrude Stein normally refused to consider an audience while she was writing, she was always a firm believer in the larger and unspecialized public for the work of art once that work was done. *Tender Buttons,* compared to cubism, has had as yet relatively little if any effect on the literary sense of the public, partly because literature has lagged behind painting, but there are many signs that if there is to be a new literature it will be one whose primary values are the real and the marvelous together and both in an extreme degree, so that

---

and objects, which joined with her first experiments done in Spain, made the volume Tender Buttons." Cf. also *Lectures in America,* p. 189.

Tender Buttons may shortly and suddenly find itself with a larger public.

Gertrude Stein, consuming problems and periods as fast as Picasso, did leave *Tender Buttons* well behind her. She decided that the proper subject of literature was man, not objects, and she also felt there had to be more movement. Nevertheless the question of what literary sense a writer is to make of objects in space, indeed what conceptual sense anyone is to make of them beyond naming them, is still and always a fundamental question, and *Tender Buttons* may stand for a long while as one of the most wonderful answers we have ever had.

Also, the human is very much present in *Tender Buttons* as the "inside." She said later that the book had been the beginning of mixing the outside with the inside, or the inside as seen from the outside, or a struggle between sight, sound, and inside.[23] And *Tender Buttons* closes with the words: "The care with which the rain is wrong and the green is wrong and the white is wrong, the care with which there is a chair and plenty of breathing. The care with which there is incredible justice and likeness, all this makes a magnificent asparagus, and also a fountain."

To commit a gloss: the continued attention to the incoherence of outside things with the previous interior version of such things, to a settled point of view and to not interrupting the natural rhythm of life, to the recognition of differences and to exact reproduction, makes a prolonged natural growth (an asparagus) or a willful direction of a natural force (the stream of consciousness has been by concentration converted into a fountain, if you like).[24] What it all

23. *The Autobiography of Alice B. Toklas,* p. 129.
24. Cf. *Geography and Plays,* p. 90. "If purpose is intellectual then there is a garden, if there is a garden there is a fountain, if there is a fountain then there is an intellectual purpose." One may add that fountains are said to play.

makes then is really an inside thing, though it is expressed and at last defined in outside terms.

The inside is continuously and operatively there as the mind of Gertrude Stein, indeed as the words and sentences themselves since they are intellectual constructions, but likewise the values, feelings, and events of human life—kind, foolish, serene, hate, pride, neglect, show, and so on—are constantly being used as a descriptive terminology. The use of them in describing inanimate objects is not a confusion or a failing of exactitude. It can be known as a very real interchange. As I said, the feeling that became very clear to Gertrude Stein in Granada, from the opposition of man to nature, was that the reality of the inside was as final as the reality of the outside, that a smile or an intonation or a feeling of misgiving, whether or not it expressed an eternal type of character, was as absolute a reality as the outline of the Sierra Nevada against the blue sky. That an intonation does not last as long as the outline of the Sierra Nevada is not relevant to the immediate and final present. All the little things that in a longer perspective of time look trivial and transient and so negligible suddenly become as real as the president of the republic or original sin or the Rock of Gibraltar, and it is quite as delightful and urgent to the mind to define these little things, any group of them given together, as to articulate a political or a theological or an imperial system.

Given this feeling or belief, anything inside or outside that "happens to come" is as it were waylaid by the consciousness of the writer, and just as it is, with the writer's feeling about it and his angle of vision, it forms a composition in itself, to be described with loving care and possessed as closely as possible. That is, if the writer is in love with everything, as Gertrude Stein was. Anything can be described roughly and loosely by the rather limited range of vocabulary conventionally applied to it, but for reproducing the exact character

88

of the experience as one has it one frequently has to draw on vocabularies which are conventionally used to describe other kinds of phenomena. As in the passage "go red go red, laugh white." This is elementary enough and everyone does a little of it. But this dislocation of vocabulary, or metaphor as we call it, is not merely a formal figure but a vitally important activity; first because it can be very much more exact than the normal vocabulary and then because it creates or realizes momentarily a unity between the inside and the outside worlds, or between any of the categories of existence, on the human basis of the word. Such a unity may be, in other arts and rites, on the basis of formalized action, as in the bullfight, or on the basis of physical absorption, as in Holy Communion, but in the course of the ritual or the work of art the human and the inhuman—the inside and the outside—are brought together, and on human terms. The meeting may be loving or hostile or simply casual and conversational, but there is a meeting and there can be an exchange.

As the quality or value of something can correspond exactly to the quality of something else on the inside or outside, the assertion of the word which represents that quality abstracted from all contexts realizes the two things, makes them exist together and exchange aspects, and creates what one may call an artistic transaction. As one may compare words to money [25]—an abstraction corresponding to exact value in any number of contexts—food, clothing, work, and

25. Cf. *The Geographical History of America* (Random House, 1936), p. 165:

> "Money is what words are.
> Words are what money is.
> Is money what words are
> Are words what money is."

There is also a nice parallel between writing and finance. At one time she thought avarice, the accumulation of sheer value and its isolation from exchange, might be a 20th century virtue. After the second World War she decided the dollar was wonderfully isolated but very lonely. And her last writing is very gregarious.

so on. And while words, like money, can be dealt with in suspension from their equivalents in reality, that is, counted and loved and hoarded, the normal realization of money is in its exchange against real goods, as real goods are realized or evaluated against money. So experience and words are evaluated and realized against each other. In *Tender Buttons* the various categories of existence meet, often enough to their complete consternation, in the word, and the meetings were for Gertrude Stein a series of very exciting realizations. For such realizations the word must be capable of a great range of applications, as the banker's dollar is capable of a great range of exchanges. Like the word "asparagus" in the passage quoted and glossed above. If an asparagus is a natural phenomenon and the notions of ethics and feelings and events are all natural phenomena too, there is no reason why a disposition of mind should not be described in vegetable terms as well as in any others, or why an asparagus should not be described in the terminology of ethics or music. As persistent or *sostenuto*. We are accustomed to tomatoes, peaches, and prunes as human types, and an extension of that usage is no great strain on the mind. Gertrude Stein used as a title "Say It with Flowers," and indeed the words for the things of any category can be used to articulate the things of any other category. There is no reason, since we do live with the whole world at once, why everything should not be brought into the same market. The world may reasonably be taken as a fair. And one is free to buy whatever strikes one's fancy. Gertrude Stein did, literally as well as metaphorically, buy very strange things, and nothing was more agitating and exciting than to go shopping with her. Reading her writing is much the same thing.

There is usually a popular or even slang precedent for the techniques used by Gertrude Stein. Her famous sentence, "Toasted susie is my icecream," is a very slight heightening of what would be popular enough: Sunburnt Susie is my

90

dish. But while "dish" is so much used in our idiom to say object of appetite that it is not even felt as a metaphor, ice cream is not so immediately perspicuous. The visibility tends to stop at the literal meaning, and really there we are. We may or we may not try to see around it or behind it, but the metaphor is meant to be taken literally, in disconnection from the experience that occasioned it. The creative process is here less one of metaphor than of metamorphosis,[26] and the resulting wonderful monster is the proper object of our attention. Susie, for our purposes, is literally toasted and ice cream. In asking for a photograph or some other recognizable version of the original dark delectable gypsy, we should be officious and far off the point. This metaphoric process, or rather this metamorphosis by words, is, with differences, a little like the distortions of Matisse in color and line or like the more complete conversions in the cubist paintings of Picasso. That is, as Matisse seeing a fairly rich curve or a pleasant spot of color in the subject matter would exaggerate these into a sumptuous curve or a gorgeous area of color on his canvas, and as Picasso would make any approximately flat or approximately angular surface in the subject matter into a very definite quadrangle on canvas, so Gertrude Stein, intensifying and converting the original qualities of the subject matter by isolation and metaphor, winds up with a result that exists in and for itself, as the paintings do. The original may or may not have been metamorphosed beyond recognition. In either case the reality is now in the expressive organization, the harmonics or interrelated detail of the work of art. The center of balance and reality is there,[27] not in its

26. Gertrude Stein said of Juan Gris (*Portraits and Prayers*), p. 46: "Juan Gris is one is the one who combines perfection with transsubstantiation." Very nearly that can be said of her own "Spanish" period.
27. One might use the word "stylization" to mean a process of abstraction which leaves the center of reality in the subject matter.

91

source. Nor in the process, which is very exciting and absorbing to the artist but not the affair of the beholder. And still the work is an exact reproduction of the original experience—that is, the subject matter plus the direct vision and emotion of the artist. Any inexactitude or falsification in vision and emotion is appreciable enough in the result, in a certain automatism of sequence or again in the quality we know as corn. In work that is not corny the vision and emotion are so closely involved in and alive to the subject matter that the essential quality of the work is very like whatever has been seen as the essential quality of the subject matter, but that does not get us as the audience anywhere. It gets the artist to making his work as real as the original, but we cannot measure the exactitude of the reproduction, we can only know that there is an authenticity, a finality, a decision in the handling of endless variables and possibilities that can only come from exact reproduction and cannot be invented. We are faced with the qualities of the thing before us, not its genesis but an independent and new thing, which we must look at and not through if we are to know it at all. We have to be, as Gertrude Stein once suggested, simple.[28] Simple as in looking at any natural phenomenon, if one has not lost the gift of looking simply, because the "tender button" is meant to be a natural phenomenon like any other, not a commentary on a phenomenon. As the painter's problem was at the time to make the picture "come out of its frame" [29] and be a thing among other things around us, with the same reality, so *Tender Buttons* does not mean to be more literature or the explanation of home life but simply something to read, as a rose is something to look at or smell or as a chair is something to sit in—independent of botany or interior decoration. Reading it depends a good deal on

28. Quoted by Thornton Wilder in his Introduction to *Four in America* (Yale University Press, 1947), p. v.

29. *Lectures in America*, p. 87.

having a sense of the word as a solid existence in itself and indeed of the concept as a reality, as constituting when it comes a place and a duration, even an event, which is the way with Latin and Spanish literature mostly but not with English. Gertrude Stein was convinced that the American language was something else again than English for any American, and she used the language not in an English way but in something like the Spanish or even the Arabian way.[30]

The created object existing in itself, in disconnection from origin and purpose and historical context, is a very natural thing in Spain, and with us a distinct theory of it follows naturally on such thought of the late 19th century as Münsterberg's definition of art as isolation, and we may say with the psychologists that the first movement of any thought, attention, is abstraction and isolation, or with current philosophy that all knowledge requires the ἐποχή or suspension of what is not the object; in short we can justify the isolated object right and left and still we may feel uneasy about it. We can perfectly feel that if all history and all theology and all science led inexorably to *Tender Buttons* the book still would not be our dish. The question really is, is an isolated thing and a disconnected thing our kind of thing? Gertrude Stein said Americans were disconnected and Henry James speaks of the American gift for disconnection,[31] but is it so and if it is so can we feel it at all clearly? Anyone who likes being up in a plane or fast driving in a car or just getting out of town in any direction or roughing it or crime or collecting stamps or the Lone Ranger, must have some feeling for it. The interest of detective stories, which Gertrude Stein liked so much, is really in the excitement of not knowing how

30. The Arabian sense seems to permit rhyming in prose, for example, and, by a very highly developed rhetoric, a calligraphy not only of the written words but of their meanings.

31. *The Ivory Tower* (Scribner's, 1917), p. 78: ". . . a vessel of the American want of correspondence . . . a special radiance of disconnection . . . "

everything really connects and centralizes until the very end, and the end is always a disappointment, no matter how hard it tries to be a surprise and a satisfaction at once. The dead part of the story is always the reconstruction of the crime, the explaining of the connections. The scientifically minded reader may like that part, but not the "simple" reader. Likewise, in the second World War the amount of logistics arranged for the fighting was immense, but the actual simple fighting was done with little if any feeling of connection to or dependence on the organization. It was natural to get lost or wander about or get surrounded and still go on with it, quite as if nothing had happened since Kit Carson and the ring of covered wagons. The disconnection of bombing planes, of artillery, of tanks, from any but the most tenuous connection with their objectives or a general situation, was vivid enough. And the trench was superseded by the fox-hole. Given that there was a war, I think most of us liked it to be that way. In any case it all goes to show that a disconnected and isolated thing can be a natural pleasure to us. Currently it is true that in the face of a more and more incoherent reality we are insisting on greater and greater organization, on interdependences and responsibilities and adjustments, so that we pay very little attention to anything but connections. And yet it is fascinating how the connections get totally isolated from what they were to connect, how responsibility and adjustment exist in themselves, not as to anything in particular, how the bell-shaped curve becomes a thing in itself with no felt connection to the data it graphs. It is quite like the distinct feeling of "and" which William James announced. So disconnection even of connections may be our national method in spite of ourselves. Most likely we prefer literature to make the connections in human life and dispose of them for us—as science takes care of the connections between things for us—while a written

94

work that behaves as we do is the last thing we expect. But then we may suddenly take to *Tender Buttons* as exactly our kind of thing, as an exact reproduction of our kind of reality.

Gertrude Stein once said that the 20th century way of doing anything was to make the cheapest things out of the best materials, because nothing less will stand the wear and tear. *Tender Buttons* was intended to be available to anybody with a grade-school education, anybody who can count up to ten with confidence, add, subtract, and divide by two. The overt intellectual operations of *Tender Buttons* are no more complicated than that. Her use of parataxis and asyndeton, which is to say "and and and," or lists with no connections is simply counting. It is a child's way of counting or telling anything, and also the way of the *Iliad,* Hesiod, the Old Testament, and medieval litanies and prayers.[32] Her constant use of *is* or *makes* as the main verb is a simple sum or equation. Again it is child's play, but the problem of one is three once split the world apart and the internal fission of the Trinity was as consequential as the fission of the atom. Again, abstraction certainly includes subtraction, and Gertrude Stein's constant question of what is the difference between one thing and another is evidently division. I do not see that she did much with multiplication, unless one cares to say that saying a thing a number of times multiplies it. At any rate these simple operations are ultimate operations

32. The list, which was for a long time a basic method for Gertrude Stein, is a counterpart of the episodic method in narrative. In *Tender Buttons* and many other works it is natural, as each moment of confrontation or exchange with the material is an absolute, that the composition be a series of absolutes, a list, a bouquet, or a collection. Once the causal continuity is broken, and the interdependencies and subordinations of a harmonic or resonant composition are foregone, the series of distinct items has to be sustained by for example a definite number or a category (as in "One Hundred Prominent Men") or by an impulse or an attitude (as with "A Bouquet" or "A Collection").

of the mind, whether they are done by the grade-school child or by Socrates. Science calls it dichotomizing but it is dividing by two, and one can have as high an old time "halving rivers and harbors" as in dividing the oviparous from the mammal and coming out with the answer that the whale is not a fish. The answers in *Tender Buttons* are even more marvelous than that. Gertrude Stein said of the book, it all came out so strangely. So that all *Tender Buttons* really requires on the part of the reader is a grade-school education and a decent liking for the marvelous. In that sense it is a cheap product, within almost anyone's intellectual means. And the trouble really is that one gets fascinated by the "very best" material out of which it is made. Gertrude Stein was forever having brilliant perceptions and extremely clever ideas, but as they grew directly out of her daily experience and were part of it they never got far in the way of an articulate system. However they do very much get into her work. She told Hemingway that remarks are not literature and she said that there is no thought in masterpieces—and it can be admitted that the composition itself should be as much as possible the only articulation of its meaning present to the reader—but in much of her own work ideas are present which are so brilliantly true that they distract and seduce one from the work itself. For example this sentence on France: "The special scenery which makes the blameless see and the solitary resemble a conversation is not that which resembles that memory." [33] I know of nothing better on the French landscape than that nor of anything better on the music of Satie than the sentence which closes Gertrude Stein's portrait of him: "It is early for all." [34] Or where will you find anything more essential on the difference between the North and the South in our Civil War, or indeed on the difference between any north and any south, than

33. *Geography and Plays*, p. 28.
34. *Portraits and Prayers*, p. 27.

"And the North in agreement with it.

As the South in an agreement with it." [35]

Or on history than "History takes time." [36]

She could not do without ideas, her work is full of them, and she was one of the most quotable writers of her time, both when she was making recognizable sense and when she was not. But she felt, as any artist feels, that even very good ideas should be dominated if not lost in the specific vitality and character of the work itself. She struggled with this problem a long time. She came to using ideas that were so obvious and commonplace that they would not disturb the work or wrench the center of gravity from within the work itself. In some of her work, like *The Geographical History of America* and *Lectures in America*, ideas are the main thing. They are expressed as they are had, that is, as a personal activity, but they are the major compositional means and quite overtly. One could make a separate study of all that, but for the moment it is enough to say that ideas or their use and place were an essential problem to her as they are bound to be to any writer in this century, indeed to anyone alive now. What is their compositional use in anything?

This literary bother about ideas in the work is something like the painter's bother about the subject matter in the painting.

I think the annoyance comes from the fact that the oil painting exists by reason of these things the oil painting represents in the oil painting, and profoundly it should not do so, so thinks the oil painting, so sometime thinks the painter of the oil painting, so instinctively feels the person looking at the oil painting. Really in everybody's heart there is a feeling of annoyance at the inevitable existence of an oil painting in

35. *Useful Knowledge* (Payson and Clarke Ltd., 1928, by permission of Harcourt, Brace), p. 19.

36. *Last Operas and Plays* (Rinehart, 1949), p. 279.

97

relation to what it has painted people, objects and land-scapes. And indeed and of course as I have already made you realize that is not what an oil painting is. An oil painting is an oil painting, and these things are only the way the only way an oil painter makes an oil painting.

One might say almost all oil painters spend their life in trying to get away from this inevitability. They struggle and the result is what everybody naturally likes or dislikes depending upon whether they think the struggle is hopeless or whether it is not. And then everybody almost everybody likes a resemblance even when there is none. Does the painter like the resemblance, oh yes he does. He does like a resemblance. That is a naturally pleasant human thing, to like a resemblance. And does this naturally pleasant human thing the liking a resemblance make everything difficult very difficult. Yes it certainly does. And it makes an oil painting annoying.[37]

A reader of *Tender Buttons* may feel something of the same annoyance, or he may try to satisfy his human liking for a resemblance. At all events the situation is a constant one and one has to do as one likes about it. Gertrude Stein said of the magpies in *Four Saints:* "They the magpies may tell their story if they or you like or even if I like but stories are only stories but that they stay in the air is not a story but a landscape." [38] The whole play being, as Gertrude Stein intended, a landscape, the magpies in the sky are simply an existence within the play, and that is the important thing. The story of the magpies, that Miss Stein saw them holding themselves flat on the sky above Avila like the bird of the Holy Ghost in early Italian Annunciation pictures, or that they are thievish and bad-tempered, or anything else, that

37. *Lectures in America,* pp. 84–85.
38. *Ibid.,* pp. 129–130.
98

is as one may happen to know it or think of it. But the play like a landscape simply exists as a small or large number of variously interrelated phenomena, an absolute and gratuitous thing in itself, as anything seems to want or like to be now.

4. Movement in Space, or Plays

Tender Buttons is a landmark in the work of Gertrude Stein, as the first uncompromising attempt to create a thing existing in itself, converting all its ingredients to its own reality. It was her first unmistakable "cake." In retrospect she could say that *The Making of Americans* existed in itself, and she was probably right, but for the reader who just comes to it from other literature and not back to it from later Stein it keeps too many naturalistic proportions and attachments to be as clearly its own reality as *Tender Buttons* is. At any rate *Tender Buttons,* written in 1911, was the first of the "incomprehensible" works on which her reputation mainly rested. The problem of *Tender Buttons,* that of a thing existing in itself, of an absolute and absolutely present literary work, was the problem which dominated all of her later writing, even when it returned to reporting and ordinary intelligibility.

The problem is after all the final one of writing, and whether or not she solved it she did constantly live in it.[1] She once said, "Think of the Bible and Homer think of

1. Cf. *Geographical History,* p. 155. "Not solve it but be in it, that is what one can say of the problem of the relation of human nature to the human mind . . ."

Shakespeare and think of me." [2] However one feels about the blithe immodesty of the remark, the fact remains that her work was written in that company, in terms of the final realities and questions of her art, as well as of her time. So that while schools and fashions may help a little in accounting for her work, the final questions and the permanent masterpieces are more to the point. It will be proper enough when I, who am concerned with Greek, try to explain her work in terms of the *Iliad* and Herodotus and Plato. I do not mean that her work is as great as the *Iliad* or that it was influenced by it in any detail, but that she wrote "from the standpoint of masterpieces." That is the scale of it, or the pitch, and any masterpieces with which the reader is familiar will serve to tune him to Gertrude Stein. Just as the unearthly Irish tenor and the lilting croon of Irish speech will help to get him next to Joyce.

One of her mottoes was "If it can be done why do it," and by forever trying to do what might be impossible she at least gave her language and the literary forms a shaking from which they are not likely to recover and which certainly woke them up. As with what she described as the painter's problem, one's immediate interest in her work depends a good deal on whether or not one thinks the struggle to create writing that exists in itself is hopeless. A whole detailed history of her part of the struggle is well beyond me, and here I only want to describe broadly what she did in a few of the major and familiar forms, the theater, the novel, and the meditation or essay.

She had two distinct periods of playwriting, an early one under the influence of Spain (from 1913 to about 1920) and a later one under the influence of the landscape around her place in Bilignin (from 1922 into the thirties). The first period is mainly represented by the plays in *Geography and Plays*, the second by the volume *Operas and Plays. Last*

2. *Ibid.,* p. 81.

Operas and Plays contains a little of everything. One may append a third period, minor but very lovely, the melodramas and the opera she did toward the end of her life, but her all-out struggles with the theatrical forms came in the earlier works.

She came at the theater in a rather roundabout way, but when she got there she went, as usual, straight for the essence of the thing. She had, except for going to an opera or two, completely forgotten the theater.

There was of course Isadora Duncan and then the Russian ballet, and in between Spain and the Argentine [la Argentina] and the bullfights and I began once more to feel something about something going on at a theatre.

And then I went back, not in my reading but in my feeling to the reading of plays in childhood, the lots of characters, the poetry and the portraits and the scenery which was always of course and ought always to be of course woods that is forests and trees and streets and windows.

And so one day all of a sudden I began to write plays.[3]

The first play, "What Happened, a Play," was written in 1913, while she was still occupied with the "rhythm of the visible world" which had dominated *Tender Buttons,* and it is to be noticed that the dancers, the ballet, and the bullfight which she mentions as giving her a feeling about something going on at a theater, are primarily visible and corporeal compositions, not verbal or, except most negligibly in the ballet, narrative.

Two things are always the same the dance and war. One might say anything is the same but the dance and war are particularly the same because one can see them. That is what

3. *Lectures in America,* p. 118.

they are for [,] that anyone living then can look at them. And games do do both they do the dance and war bull-fighting and football playing, it is the dance and war anything anybody can see by looking is the dance and war. That is the reason that plays are that, they are the thing anybody can see by looking.[4]

Taking the theater from this end, that is as a physical thing going on in space, she was able later to compose eminently stageable things, but most of the plays of the first period are, I think, literary and not for the stage, though they might be very interesting on the radio. In this period a number of people or things or even ideas presenting themselves together as existences in space constituted a play. "I concluded that anything that was not a story could be a play and I even made plays in letters and advertisements." To such an extent could the text in itself be the play, so that many of them might go well on the radio, but not I think on the stage, because the visible things in the text would very often be vitiated by the visible things on the stage. However, that is a small matter, and one may live to see anything. One would hardly have expected, from reading the text, the stage success of *Four Saints*.[5]

When they were written, the idea of these earliest plays was to bring a greater liveliness, a greater movement and exchange into the "thing existing in itself" as it had been created in *Tender Buttons*. As an American she had both an impulse for complete immobility and an impulse for very fast movement of an extremely detached kind, that is a movement which depends neither on occasion nor situa-

4. *Everybody's Autobiography*, pp. 195–196.
5. *Everybody's Autobiography*, p. 318: "I hope sometime they will do one as a play [that is, not as a ballet or an opera]. I wonder can they." p. 75: ". . . he [Maurice Grosser] had a way of knowing how it was possible to play the plays that I have written."

103

tion,[6] like the movement of a plane or a fast automobile or, often enough, the movies. In the instance of the plane there is a strange combination of immobility and the utmost in movement, and it seems to satisfy American feeling, but we also certainly like a wandering and discursive movement. In a way it is these two feelings about movement that distinguish the two major periods of her playwriting. The first is based largely on Spanish movement, which is very intense, inclined to the vertical and a very narrow field. It is essentially vibration and a constant reversion to the beginning, it has very little development or wandering or discursiveness. What little wandering there is, as with *Don Quijote* or the *Cid* or the picaresque novel, is mainly there to sustain or provoke the vibration. The second period, based mainly on France, was concerned with a more complex, discursive, wandering, conversational movement. But it should be said that the Spanish dynamics continued, if not in her plays, in her poetry, where the composition gradually became one of sheer vibration and movement returning upon itself, albeit she no longer sustained the vibration upon the corporeal, as the Spanish normally do, but simply upon the substantive, the noun. As in "a rose is a rose is a rose is a rose"—a poem which she very reasonably made into a ring.

But the early plays are, as movement in space, thoroughly corporeal. Many of them are like *Tender Buttons*, one of them being called "Scenes. Actions and Dispositions of Relations and Positions." Another, written as late as 1922,

6. Cf. *Lectures in America*, pp. 165–166, in particular the passage: ". . . and we in America have tried to make this thing a real thing, if the movement, that is any movement, is lively enough, perhaps it is possible to know that it is moving even if it is not moving against anything." As with a plane, or as the movement of her own work is usually not realized against a known subject matter.

is called "Objects Lie on a Table." But while the outside is very persistently there in the plays it is there as it is lived in and lived with by the "vibrant" inside, which she had come back to after *Tender Buttons* as the proper subject of writing. In "A Long Gay Book" she had begun to demonstrate the inside by "little ways," gestures and actions involving the outside somewhat, and she had tried to relate various insides to each other, in pairs and threes and so on. In a way a play was a solution to all these problems. "I came to think that since each one is that one and that there are a number of them each one being that one, the only way to express this thing each one being that one and there being a number of them knowing each other was in a play. . . . And the idea in What Happened, A Play was to express this without telling what happened, in short to make a play the essence of what happened." [7]

One is not at all invited to figure out what happened. The purpose of suppressing the explicit event is to let the participants with their little ways of saying things and seeing things be the substance of what is there. Yet, again, there is no intention of "character drawing"—the characters are barely distinguishable and are often introduced as "one" or "he," or in couples as "two," or in larger anonymous groups as "the chorus." They are there really more as dancers are there. A dancer dances with or without an event and his character is of no interest. He has an impulse and enormously a style, and a lot of dancers or a pair of dancers together make a composition of physical movements in changing relation to each other, and that is all anybody asks of the dance in the way of occasion or subject matter.

The same conversion from consequential action to movement, from information to actuality, and from character to style exists in war and in games, which were frequently

7. *Lectures in America,* p. 119.

enough Gertrude Stein's models of composition.[8] In each of these there is a detachment or at least a transposition of realities from the practical complex of causalities and proportions and necessities we normally live in. The sportive motivation is a constant one, in the composition of comedies and also of tragedies—it commands the *Iliad* and the *Oedipus* as it commands Aristophanes—indeed one may seriously suspect it of being the deepest and certainly the most human motivation in art. As with the use of metaphor as I described it in the last chapter, war, sport, the dance, and games all bring the human and the inhuman together on terms that are gratuitously chosen by the human will and impulse. In any case, Gertrude Stein made the most of the verbal coincidence between plays and play.[9]

With some reservations it can be said that the plays of this period are ballets of concepts and perceptions, as one might say Pope's *Essay on Man* is a minuet of adages or that Swinburne is the Offenbach of sentimental ideation. The ballet is clear to us and so may help to understand, but in the time of the plays Gertrude Stein could work also from her sense of the melodramas of her youth [10] or the silent films,[11] where the essential thing is or was the immediate physical movement, not the character drawing or the plot or the message. She meant them as plays, not as ballets or movies or whatever, but as plays they have far more in

8. E.g., "I will be ordered like the American Army and I will like it." *Operas and Plays*, p. 128.

9. E.g., *Geographical History*, p. 119:
"   Play I
The Human mind.
The human mind at play."

10. When very young she wrote a melodrama called "Snatched from Death, or, The Sundered Sisters." It is interesting that among her last plays are small melodramas for children.

11. Cf. *Lectures in America*, p. 104. She did not copy cinema techniques but she was conscious of having problems in common with the movies. She wrote "A Movie" in 1920.

common with those forms than with say Ibsen. In the next period, when the play is replaced by the opera, this choreographic quality of the composition becomes perfectly clear, as we are used to a tradition of anonymous voices, an uninformative dialogue, and the absence of a plot or a plot so melodramatic one can forget it. Her operas do take music and staging very well,[12] but they are first of all literary works embodying the essential qualities of the opera—lyrical dramas, if you will—as her plays are literary works embodying the essence of stage plays.

While a play is composed in space, the dimension that was being explored by Gertrude Stein when she began writing plays, what really kept her fascinated was that the theatrical event, whether a ballet or a dance or a bullfight or an opera or a play, does create a thing existing in itself. The stage reality is, for the duration of the play, *the* reality. While many of its elements are recognizable as being the same as in life, the stage reality does not live by that recognition but by the movement of relationships on the stage. The audience is kept from remembering anything outside the play by the simple pressure of stage time, which can very easily be a continuous present, impose its material in isolation and directly, and fix the attention. In telling about the cubist décor which Picasso painted for the ballet *Parade,* Gertrude Stein said: "When a work is put on the stage everyone is forced to look and since they are forced to look at it, of course, they must accept it, there is nothing else to do." [13] This advantage in right projection which stage space afforded Picasso's painting she supposed that simple stage time would afford her writing. I believe radio time is clearer for her writing,[14] but she did after all write with

12. *Four Saints* and *The Mother of Us All* were written with production in mind but they do not greatly differ in manner from the other operas which have been only printed.

13. *Picasso,* p. 29.

14. The radio production of *Four Saints* made the verbal ele-

107

the stage in mind and the dominant conception was movement in space. The stage tradition of a progressive fatality or of suspense had complicated and confused simple stage time, but she restored simple stage time by simply not having a plot. Vaudeville, burlesque, and the Broadway review had an all but simple stage time but used it in a very limited range of expression. Comedy, living as it does on present disconnection and the nonsequitur, might have done something immense at the time, but on the whole it confined itself to the drawing room or the bedroom, or, as with Shaw, for all his command of the stage, to off-stage issues. Probably the Marx brothers did the most with the possibilities.

It is a not very remarkable coincidence that Henry James too, that absolute Racine of the American novel, had been fascinated with the possibilities the stage offered for an isolated and self-sustaining composition. In his preface to *The Awkward Age* he runs through the conventional objections to the theater as being an impossible vehicle for an idea of the least subtlety, and then goes on to explain that the theater is essentially no such vehicle in the first place:

He [the spectator] is to be caught at the worst in the act of attention, of the very greatest attention, and that is all, as a precious preliminary at least, that the playwright asks of him, besides being all the very divinest poet can get. I remember rejoicing as much to remark this, after getting launched in "The Awkward Age," as if I were in fact constructing a play; just as I may doubtless appear now not less anxious to keep the philosophy of the dramatist's course before me than if I belonged to his order. I felt, certainly, the support he feels, I participated in his technical amuse-

---

ment extremely clear and real, while the more exciting stage production did not isolate and impose it in that way. Which is preferable depends on the attention of the audience, which notoriously changes from season to season.

108

*ment, I tasted to the full the bitter-sweetness of his draught
—the beauty and the difficulty (to harp again on that
string) of escaping poverty even though the references in
one's action can only be, with intensity, to each other, to
things exactly on the same plane of exhibition with themselves. Exhibition may mean in a "story" twenty different
ways, fifty excursions, alternatives, excrescences, and the
novel, as largely practised in English, is the perfect para-
dise of the loose end. The play consents to the logic of but
one way, mathematically right, . . . We are shut up wholly
to cross-relations, relations all within the action itself; no
part of which is related to anything but some other part—
save of course by the relation of the whole to life. . . . All
of which was to make in the event for complications.*[15]

The "dramatist's philosophy" and his commitment to a
single plane of exhibition are what direct the composition
in the literary plays of Gertrude Stein. They may seem to
be entirely composed of loose ends, because the relationship which connects each little bit to another little bit is
not the usual narrative or active relationship but a simple
"theatrical" relationship. None of the words is intended to
suggest a context outside the text. For example, this early
play, "A Curtain Raiser," is a small vaudeville made of numbers and a few qualities, behaving according to the stage
or page reality, not as they behave off stage or off page.

A CURTAIN RAISER

*Six.
Twenty.
       Outrageous.
Late,
Weak.
       Forty.*

15. *The Art of the Novel* (Scribner's, 1934), pp. 113–114.

More in any wetness.
Sixty three certainly.
Five.
Sixteen.
Seven.
Three.
More in orderly.   Seventy-five.[16]

Here the simple mention of things one after the other
—the sequence being no more than an irregular alternation of quantities and qualities, with an arbitrary diminish-
ing and increasing of numbers out of all numerical sequence
—has replaced the much more complex progressions of
Tender Buttons, which had been so deeply involved in all
the qualities of the visible world. Here she has extricated
herself by sacrificing almost everything to the immediate
and intrinsic movement. The things that move are not connected with each other naturally, any more than a seal is
naturally connected with a tin horn, or a bowl of goldfish
with a silk hat, but their arbitrary association can be made
the basis of a charming little performance.

"A Curtain Raiser" is a very uncomplicated act by merely
numbers and qualities moving on what I have tried to define as a Spanish dynamics, but Gertrude Stein let almost
anything get into her acts: descriptions, spoken things, letters, advertisements, aphorisms, people, and a host of little
incidents that came up in her daily life and showed promise
for the page. The promise was largely in the way they
moved, in the overt quality of their existence. She looked at
everything with something of the eye of a talent scout,
and Matisse was about right when he said she was only interested in theatrical values.

In the first play, "What Happened, a Play," descriptions
quite like those in *Tender Buttons* are used to compose the

16. *Geography and Plays,* p. 202.
110

act, but the descriptions are said by groups of "characters" or, better, seen by a number of insides.

(*The same three*)
A wide oak a wide enough oak, a very wide cake, a lightning cooky, a single wide open and exchanged box filled with the same little sac that shines.
The best the only better and more left footed stranger.
The very kindness there is in all lemons oranges apples pears and potatoes.[17]

Each of the three parts here has a distinct style and personality, though it requires some sensitivity and a total attention perhaps to distinguish them. If one were to cast painters for the parts, one might assign Braque to the first, Marcel Duchamp for the second, and Bonnard to the third, and they would not be at all interchangeable. Not that the painters had anything to do with it in reality, but the differences of style are quite real. In other plays, where the material is less rich or not so visual, I often find I have not the force of attention or the sensitivity to appreciate fully such differences and the essential quality of the movement, but here I think it is all obvious enough.

Also one can appreciate well enough the sequences, tones, manners, and movements in this passage from "Ladies' Voices":

Act II
Honest to God Miss Williams I don't mean to say that I was older.
But you were.
Yes I was. I do not excuse myself. I feel that there is no reason for passing an archduke.
You like the word.

17. *Ibid.*, pp. 206–207.

111

You know very well that they all call it their house.
As Christ was to Lazarus so was the founder of the hill to
Mahon.
You really mean it.
I do.[18]

And the following passage from "For the Country Entirely," which combines letters, dialogue, a vivid plastic,
and even an incident, offers no difficulty.

Scene 6

Dear Sir. Remember that when you have no further requests
to make you must not blame me.
Dear Sir. I know you do not object to smoke.
Dear Mrs. Lindo Webb How can you break your teeth.
By falling down in the street.
You mean now when the pavement is so dark.
Naturally.
It would not have happened otherwise.
This is because of the necessary condition of lighting.
We all suffer from that.[19]

So it goes, for a great many plays in the volume *Geography
and Plays*, and most of them make very easy and entertain-
ing reading, only provided one reads them as one would
watch a vaudeville or a ballet, without expecting them to
make any sense but their own, without wondering about
the life of Mrs. Lindo Webb before she went on the page.

Speaking more largely, with *Three Lives* and *The Making of Americans* Gertrude Stein had gradually reduced
time to a simple present, and had destroyed history and
narrative sequence as the dominating element in literature,
which they had been in the 19th century. With *Tender*

18. *Ibid.*, p. 203.
19. *Ibid.*, p. 236.

Buttons she had entered space, and within the limited if universal field of the household she had made an articulate thing of the direct relations of the inside to things in space. But *Tender Buttons* was limited, like the still lifes of painters, and while it stands by the extraordinary force of its concentration, like cubist paintings, it served Gertrude Stein rather as an opening wedge into a broader art.

As all inhabited time is history, and as *The Making of Americans,* as broad as it is long, had extracted the essence of all human history, a broader art of space was going to have to come sooner or later to geography, whether as places and scenery or as all inhabited space, still as an immediate and final term of human existence within the present.[20] Gertrude Stein had so strongly the sense of spatial reality that what made death make sense to her was the consideration that if people did not die there would be no room for other generations to come and live in. One may say that most of her work, from *Geography and Plays* on, was dominated by space. Not only in such works as *The Geographical History of America* and *The World Is Round,* but in the whole mentality and method of her later narratives, essays, and plays. Even her conception of time became spatialized, that is, she said the American thing in literary composition was a space of time filled with movement, and it can be said of even her very disembodied "vibrant" poetry of the later periods that it rests on at least empty space, insofar as a vibration is a motion that stays in place.

In the early works, however, she tried a great many ways of composing a thing in ordinary space. She used doorways and windows as natural divisions or frames of a composition, or she used pages as the unit of writing.

20. Cf. *Lucy Church Amiably:* "In every instance there is a difference between history and geography." P. 16. That is, anything has the two aspects, both reasonably final. At this time she was simply choosing to insist on the spatial aspect.

113

She used nations as landscapes in describing people. Or she used capital cities and villages. Or she used the movement and amount of traffic in the streets or on the roads as a basis of composition. The landscape, with everything going on in it or being in it, is eminently suited for description in a continuous present, since on the whole it is not going anywhere, it is just there, and the things that move in it do not move but are simply included in its present existence. Present movement within a space, or space, or a space of time became her ultimate reality, as it was the reality of the movies and of America generally. But taking it deliberately as the first condition and the last orientation of writing and of plays brought her into direct contradiction with the traditional theory of drama.

Aristotle of course took up the drama at exactly the other end, as a progressive action or story with an ethical or emotional orientation—a sort of therapeutic exhaustion of public emotions in the interest no doubt of a rational polity. For him, motion in space was the least significant of the elements of the drama. His theory has next to nothing to do with the Greek drama and really little enough to do with anything on the stage later, but it has tended to becloud criticism rather seriously. Drama is still conceived as leading up to and then easing off from a climax or paroxysm, in short as the modulation of consequences. Gertrude Stein very happily analyzed the use of this scheme as resulting simply in confusion and nervousness on the part of the audience. Indeed nervousness and anxiety are the consecrated emotions of the theater, even of most comedy, and certainly for Aristotle the tragic drama was to deal in fear and pity and other such passions—or what we now like to call *Angst*. One may feel that even the tragic theater should offer more than the pleasure of working up to and recovering from a bad fright, but, if it should, the consequential time of the drama has to be destroyed or at least

114

seriously tampered with. And if one cuts through it to the simple present which is there and given, one has to use articulations which are primarily choreographic and spatial—that is, it must all be conceived as immediate movement and not as action involving causes, projects, and results; and as the juxtaposition of qualities rather than as events following each other. Drama is as naturally made of the shocks of confrontation, of association or dissociation in the present instant, of sudden changes and interruptions, of the movement of several insides and outsides in relation to each other, as of the destruction of all this by a general movement of everything away from the present into the future. The general movement does drag the audience along with it, there is no doubt about it, and plenty of people like to be agitated and swept away, but Gertrude Stein was right enough when she pointed out that the emotion of an ordinary stage climax is essentially relief, that is, a relief over having at last caught up with the heart of the matter. She meant instead to create something in which the heart of the matter would be constantly there, as with dancing or bullfighting or such modern painting as maintains an equal interest over every inch of the surface. And she did. She meant the emotion to be continuous delight, as at a circus, not Angst, no matter how serious her subject or her thinking got to be.

The use of simple stage time had already been approached by Chekhov, and it was to come later in the American plays on the basis of the hotel or the screwball household or the barroom, where the vitality of the stage event is entirely in the variety of little encounters rather than in the large action. Gertrude Stein simply carried the principle much further, into the sequence of words and ideas as well as the sequence of action. Naturally she did not solve the whole problem of the theater in the 20th century once and for all, and many kinds of solutions are no doubt possible, even

115

with consequential action; but it is probably true that the theater now has in general only two choices of basic composition—either inconsequential movement in space, like the ballet, or melodrama maintaining a continuous crisis, varied by tirades and prodigies and the like, in the manner of Corneille and Calderón.

It is worse than no use being heavy-handed with the little "Curtain Raiser" quoted above,[21] but it does make a good example, and it shows clearly how Gertrude Stein's use of numbers is a pretty good key to the behavior of the other elements in the composition. The numbers mentioned there are not a progressive sequence but various arbitrary quantities that turn up on the page rather as odd groups of things, smaller or larger than each other, turn up before the attention in a landscape, whether the groups be of flowers or people or hills or sheep. In "A Curtain Raiser" the odd qualities turn up in disconnection from all historical situation just as the numbers turn up in disconnection from arithmetical order. But together they compose as experience composes. For instance, if you should notice there are six sheep over there and twenty trees and a very lurid sunset with it all, you might feel it as a wonderful and exciting composition. It has no mechanical or active coherence but rather a qualitive coherence, and then simply that these things should come together there before you in space is somehow a surprise and a pleasure. The literary composition:

Six

Twenty

Outrageous

21. Gertrude Stein said of it (*Lectures in America*, p. 119): "I did this last because I wanted still more to tell what could be told if one did not tell anything." She told even less in "Are There Six or Another Question" (*Useful Knowledge*, p. 83), which is as absolute as Mondriaan.

which after all does oppose and juxtapose a pleasant difference or increase between small pluralities to a violent fluid thing just as the sheep and trees and sunset might, can stand without further articulation, insofar as spatial juxtaposition or confrontation within the present is, in this art, a final articulation, as in painting. The normal composition of narrative—"and then and then and then," or "because," or "and so"—makes its fundamental sense by our necessary habit of seeing things in consequential juxtaposition, and anything whatever can be finally articulated with anything else as long as the consequence is maintained. For instance if we say, "A leaf flapped at the window. She screamed. Her cigarette fell to her knees and burnt a bistre stain in the white satin," all these heterogeneous things are given a final articulation together just by being together in consequence and action. But in existence and in experience things are together in a time or a space whether there is any action or not, and that juxtaposition or simultaneity is perfectly real and if not so sympathetic and provocative as a consequence or a story still quite as intelligible. "A Curtain Raiser" is quite like the juxtaposition, counterpoise, change, and tension of colors, lines, and shapes, in a "passage" in painting. "A Curtain Raiser" happens to correspond to the extremely simple and dry and tense cubist drawings done by Picasso at the same time (1913), but the final articulation is the same as that of any drawing or painting that is really composed and not only representing. Gertrude Stein said much later that her middle writing was painting, and this is true even when no objects are mentioned.[22] Her theater is essentially visual and spectacular rather than dramatic in the sense of action.

The "interest" of these plays is a purely spectacular interest. In a theater anything that can be seen going on about its own business is interesting. When it addresses the

22. *Everybody's Autobiography*, p. 180.

audience even indirectly it is not so interesting. That is, a message, or making the stage interest mainly of things that in life impose their interest automatically, may be important and agitating enough, but not fascinating. Gertrude Stein as a woman understood fascination perfectly, and these plays of hers do not tell you anything, they merely present themselves, like a dance or a circus or any play that is really a stage play. They do not conceal anything, they do not recede from the "plane of exhibition," and yet they draw and hold the attention simply by their own force of existence. That they have nothing outside of themselves to say should not be disturbing, even in literary plays, because no literature, once you are out of school and have heard everything, is interesting for what it has to say. Only for the way it is —which may or may not include being informative.

All this leads to a very pleasant coincidence. One of the notorious devices of Aeschylus, who was all stage, was the presentation of a mute, immobile, and unaccountable personage. When the figure finally broke into speech it was still all but incomprehensible. The same device was used in the production of *Four Saints*—the Negro Saint Ignatius was kneeling and mute in the midst of the excitement for a very long time. This was due to Frederick Ashton, who was a child in Peru, and in staging *Four Saints* used an Indian sense of immobility and processions.[23] And Americans in general are finally coming to the same style of immobility and movement the Indians had and have. Gertrude Stein remarked that even in the first World War the American soldiers impressed the French enormously simply by standing and doing nothing, and that now American dancing is settling down to barely moving in place.[24] So that while the dynamics of her plays of the Spanish period may be essentially American, they coincide with and can be seen against

23. *Ibid.*, pp. 315–316.
24. *Ibid.*, pp. 197–198.
118

the Spanish theater and against what one may call the archaic Greek theater of Aeschylus, based on a constancy of verbal and scenic excitement rather than on progress of action. All three of them are so to speak vertical theater, or if you will, a fountain.

Some of the plays, since they do go on in dialogue, may seem to be getting somewhere, but it is not quite so. Gertrude Stein's favorite piece of dialogue, which kept cropping up in her work for many years, was

How do you do.
Very well I thank you.

This, like numbers, may be taken as a norm in her work. It is not informative and it certainly makes little enough of action and character drawing. It merely presents a meeting, or an exchange. Everyone knows that dramatic dialogue should be not so much about anything, that is exposition, as a presentation of the relations of the speakers to something or to each other. It is the motion and emphasis of the exchange that matters, and in very dramatic dialogue the action and character are only there to give a style and range of quality to the verbal event, to reinforce and explain it if necessary rather than to be revealed by it. Dialogue can be a verbal dance, and very frequently is, in Shakespeare for example, but most clearly, I believe, and resting on a minimum of situation and character so that it can be entirely itself, in Marivaux. Gertrude Stein said once that the French theater created a thing existing in itself, and certainly Marivaux is the quintessence of French theater. What with naturalism and realism and psychology in the 19th century Marivaux lost his reputation and *marivaudage* was a word for coy and idle patter, but now in the 20th century his greatness is coming into sight again. At any rate I mean it as both accurate and laudatory to call

119

some of these early plays of Gertrude Stein and all of her later plays marivaudage. It describes the dialogue, of course, but also the treatment of all the elements. It describes the plays as play, as an unnecessary activity, as a pure pleasure in movement.

The dangers of such a calligraphic or melodic treatment of the verbal movement are obvious. It can easily fall into sheer decoration, into being just very cantabile and no more. For example, when the dialogue of Noel Coward or Hemingway goes weak, it is usually where they are riding along too happily on this quality. Gertrude Stein sometimes did yield to that temptation and got drunk with her own melody,[25] but she did sober up and tell herself that melody and beauty should be by-products and not the substance of the work.[26]

In 1922, though her playwriting had continued off and on all along, getting mixed with poetry and games, she wrote what she considered the real beginning of her conception of a play as a landscape, "Lend a Hand or Four Religions." It was also the beginning of her writing plays with a clearly dominating melodiousness. While the plays written before and during the first World War were very strongly influenced by Spain and Mallorca, the new plays and operas are very much influenced by the south of France, first Saint Remy and later Bilignin. The change is not absolute, and she did revert to the Spanish landscape as subject matter and as a principle of composition in *Four Saints*,[27]

25. *Lectures in America,* pp. 197–199.
26. *Ibid.*, p. 201.
27. The case of *Four Saints* is exceptional. She wrote it in the spring of 1927, just before the composition of *Lucy Church Amiably,* which is very romantic and full of French landscape. *Four Saints* represents the culmination and exhaustion of the Spanish matter and spirit in Gertrude Stein. It was written in Paris and some of the material was picked up in Parisian shop windows, but it is essentially Spanish. As a Chinese painter turns away from a mountain and then looks back at it in order to see it clearly, so

but the change is there, and it means that the composition after the French landscape (even if not that of the Ile de France) would have people living in and with the landscape rather than against it or in equation to it as in Spain. As she had said, the solitary in a French landscape resembles a conversation. This ease of relationship between the human and the natural elements of the composition brought her very naturally to her novel of romantic nature, *Lucy Church Amiably,* but it also led to plays.

One of the reasons for the change was certainly the post-war. She said that after a war everyone has to get quiet again, and after the great concentration of *Tender Buttons* and the plays of the first period she was now impelled less to a still greater intensity than to what she called "distribution and equilibration." [28] Evidently, for the creation of such a thing France was the proper country and landscape, not Spain.

The easy existence together of unlikely things and of likely things is the basis of the following passage from "Lend a Hand or Four Religions." It is profoundly a French reality, and was very probably what drew so many American writers to France during the twenties. There was the

Gertrude Stein seems to have turned away from Spain and then looked back, from Paris, and saw it very clearly—though really for the last time.

The French element in the opera—aside from such small matters as the name Thérèse for Teresa—is primarily in the *lateral* movement. The saints are presented as founding and conventual, and not in vertical ecstasies à la Greco. This lateralism does exist also in Spain, for example in the great wall of Avila, but it does not involve progress and consequences. A composition in width by Velàsquez does not progress as would a similar composition by say Rubens. Each detail of the space stays in place. One may say that *Four Saints* is specifically Castilian, based on the plateau like Avila and the Escorial, not on Granada or Mallorca as were the plays of the first period. Still, it was no doubt her habit of France that made her, so to say, change Spains.

28. *Composition as Explanation,* p. 27.

same variety and improbable disorder in America, but the writers required a tradition of living in such a thing naturally and without intellectual confusion.

First religion   She is feeling that the grasses grow four times yearly and does she furnish a house as well. . . . Let her think of a stable man and a stable can be a place where they care for the Italians every day. And a mission of kneeling there where the water is flowing kneeling, a chinese christian, and let her think of a stable man and wandering and a repetition of counting. Count to ten. He did. He did not. Count to ten. And did she gather the food as well. Did she gather the food as well. Did she separate the green grasses from one another. They grow four times yearly. Did she see some one as she was advancing and did she remove what she had and did she lose what she touched and did she touch it and the water there where she was kneeling where it was flowing. And are stables a place where they care for them as well.[29]

One might say that the essence of this passage is the phrase "as well"—a sort of welcome to anything that is there to come into the composition, such a welcome being the genius of France and as often as not of America. The coherence of the passage, which consists in a sort of melodic progress of consideration, is between the rational French discursiveness and the rambling American sympathy as Whitman had it. But more important is the kind of existence expressed here. The existence of the woman in the passage is intimately involved with the existence, growth, and movement of things in the landscape. Her kneeling and the water flowing and the grass growing four times yearly and the caring for Italians are all part of the same slow natural living of the place and the world. This sense of continuity

29. *Useful Knowledge*, p. 174.

between human life and the life of the world is also in the *Iliad,* in the circus, in the Orient, and particularly in certain varieties of Christian religiosity. St. Francis' feeling of brotherhood with the sun and all of God's creatures, his preaching to the birds, is the most obvious instance, and he was one of Gertrude Stein's favorite saints, but she went in heavily at this period for all sorts of saints, militant, founding, contemplative. A saint, whether he does anything or not, exists in and with the universe and shares its life, sustained in existence by the general miracle of the present world. St. Teresa's remark, "Among the cooking pots moves the Lord," is perhaps the most vivid statement of that. The basis of this intimate exaltation over living with the life of the world was of course not, with Gertrude Stein, the Holy Spirit as in Christian theology, even when she used Christian saints and symbols to articulate what she meant, but rather a vital and radical *poetic* attitude or intuition, rather like that of Whitman.

This alliance of the poet with religion, by the way, can be confusing. It is an ancient and anthropological alliance, witness the shaman, the bard, the *vates,* but it is much more. Its permanent utility is not at all that it gives poetry a reality by the consecration of religion, but that religion, whose reality is already more real than historical or practical reality, serves very well as a working basis or springboard for the creation of an art which is also more real than history. For example, the gods of Homer do not at all authenticate the *Iliad,* but by way of the immortal muse Homer was able to reach a "divine" point of view, more exalted, more vivid, more complete, from which to compose a reality that is more real than either history or his gods. Even Aristotle was not confused about that. Homer's remark to the effect that the purpose of human history is that later generations may have a song, is a thoroughly professional remark, not naïve, and from the poet's point of view very true. And it would not have been difficult for the highhanded poet of the *Iliad* to make the same remark about his gods. We can make it, and indeed from the non-Christian point of view Christianity is real mainly by reflection from the prodigiously real art it has served to produce.

At any rate, as Homer used the point of view of the muse, Gertrude Stein used the point of view of the saint, and to the same end, the creation of a more real reality.

Aside from this, the saints have been made into immensely articulate ideas and attitudes, distinguished from the heresies and pathologies which resemble them, and still allowing great variation, and the whole system is a useful metaphor for the criticism of literature. One can assign writers to orders, as Gertrude Stein to the Carmelites, Joyce to the Jesuits or the Dominicans, and e. e. cummings to the Franciscans as a very unconventual *giullare di Dio*. And one could work out a nice dispute over martyrdom, since there is a vogue for literary martyrs and they are easily confused with saints.

While Gertrude Stein did amuse herself with such critical games and live with disciplines and temptations like a saint, the Christian saints were primarily useful to her as they afforded a stable metaphor on which to maintain and sustain her own generically poetic exaltation, her own vision of a world saturated with miracles.

But the accurate expression of such a thing is difficult. Remarks and discourse, even dramatic discourse, are not really up to it. Whitman had to sound his barbaric yawp and Gertrude Stein proceeded gradually to the opera. She had written "Talks to Saints. Or Stories of Saint Remy," but the fuller expression had to approximate prayer and singing. After all a saint may chat but when he is really being a saint he is praying or singing a hymn of praise. Before the great solution of this problem, in the opera *Four Saints in Three Acts* (1927), she had given exhaustive study to the

124

behavior of words in various kinds of projection. She had written "Practice in Orations," "Studies in Conversation," "Praises," [30] "A Hymn," "Precepts," and so on. She had also come to understand very well what she meant by a play —that is, movement in a space or in a landscape—and all that remained to be settled before a really operatic work could be written was the very bothersome question of music.

She was of course struggling with the temptations of sheer melodiousness, and she even wrote literary "sonatinas" and a pastoral, but the deeper problem was of making words have the expressive movement and "vibration" of musical sounds—not only of course in the overt sound and metric of the words but in the composition of their meanings as well. Naturally, if the words and ideas are felt to be, like the mind using them, alive and in motion, and if moreover they are to express a state of mind that takes readily to singing, the terms of musical composition are a likely help or analogy for composing them. To take an obvious example from a somewhat later work, in which the analogy of staccato is used to emphasize, isolate, and make more "vibrant" a word or a small group of words at a time:

Josephine. Josephine is called. And she has. Displaced
Xenobie. Also. She has well said. That. She
will not stay. That is. She. May be. There.
All. Are. Pleased.[31]

Here, the very simple analogy and the very simple device of punctuation have provided another means, like the line of poetry, for getting around the everlasting awkwardness of having to "phrase" our thinking by the whole sen-

30. It is worth pointing out that poetry of this kind is par excellence a Franciscan thing. The earliest Franciscan songs were called *laudi*, proceeding fairly directly out of St. Francis' vision of the world, and the first one directly out of one of his visions.

31. *Operas and Plays*, p. 165.

tence. Briefly, the advantage of using a musical analogy is a properly literary advantage, a gain in literary expressiveness.[32] It is not at all that the device is justified by having been a normal musical device, even if music is the most absolute of the arts, and can be said to govern the others if one feels that way about it. Gertrude Stein definitely did not. But she did find many pseudomusical devices very serviceable, at least during the twenties, when her work was conceived as a composition of motions.

Still her principal formal resources were, like her subject matter, drawn as directly as possible from life, not the other arts. She says in the *Autobiography of Alice B. Toklas:*

She was much influenced by the sound of the streets and the movement of automobiles. She also liked then [1921] to set a sentence for herself as a sort of tuning fork and metronome and then write to that time and tune.[33]

* * * * *

It was this summer [1922] that Gertrude Stein, delighting in the movement of the tiny waves on the Antibes shore, wrote the Completed Portrait of Picasso, the Second Portrait of Carl Van Vechten, [etc.] [34]

* * * * *

She says that listening to the rhythm of his [her dog Basket's] water drinking made her recognise the difference

32. Also of course in aptitude for musical extension or accompaniment. The work from which the last quotation was taken, "They Must. Be Wedded. To Their Wife," was later revised and used as a libretto for the ballet "A Wedding Bouquet." But the work is essentially governed by a literary concern for breaking up or cutting through the discursive or "melodic" continuity, which was threatening to become as restful and easy and dead as narrative continuity.

33. p. 171.

34. p. 184.

126

*between sentences and paragraphs, that paragraphs are
emotional and that sentences are not.*[35]

Naturally the sources of such "musical" effects cannot
be recognized through the text, it is only illuminating that
she could use as a compositional principle almost anything
she found before her, and again that she was always on
such marvelously good terms with everything in the world
around her. Picking up rhythmical means from the wave-
lets at Antibes might be natural in a painter, say Dufy, or
a composer; but it can seem like the most rarefied preciosity
in a writer unless one remembers how thoroughly Gertrude
Stein had come to live in the real present, where everything that came before her was attended to, not in a provisory way but completely, and with the finality of a Last
Judgment. Anyone who ever met her must remember the
direct innocence of her glance, how it flattered and appalled
one at once by making one for the moment the most interesting thing in the world. That the same glance was turned
on waves and automobiles and pigeons only means that she
had herself reached a kind of secular sanctity which makes of
Four Saints perhaps her most full and personal expression.
Her little description of what saints are about may be used
exactly of her:

> *They have to be.*
> *They have to be.*
> *They have to be to see.*
> *To see to say.*
> *Laterally they may.*[36]

She had to be, that is fully present and alive to whatever was there, in order really to see it as it was and then
to say it. And this activity of the artist as of the saint, and

35. p. 204.
36. *Operas and Plays*, p. 47.

indeed as the properly human activity of anybody, need not involve itself in relations like beyond or upward as in a Greco or onward as in progress, but may be complete by lateral relations as in a landscape: roundabout and in and out and left and right—as with the ring-around-a-rosy and croquet that the saints do in the opera—in the present space of this world.[37] The saints are presented not in their relation to a god but as founding orders and convents and being around and moving in the world, or just the Spanish landscape. To the Spanish saint the world is surrounded and saturated by God and the Grace of God, and Gertrude Stein is not far from this same sense of the pervading miracle in seeing everything as absolute present existence to the human mind, indeed as within the knowing of the human mind. "Foundationally marvellously aboundingly illimitably with it as a circumstance" [38] is an accurate description of either the Holy Ghost or the human mind. And with things going on at this pitch of beatitude there has to be singing and a reckless gaiety, which is very common in saints. It is alien to the fairly saintless Protestant tradition —and William James for example was exasperated by the coquettishness of Saint Teresa in relation to her Lord [39]—but

37. Cf. *Everybody's Autobiography*, p. 86. "I am also fond of saying that a war or fighting is like a dance because it is all going forward and back, and that is what everybody likes they like that forward and back movement, that is the reason that revolutions and Utopias are discouraging they are up and 'down and not forward and back."

38. *Four Saints in Three Acts*, in *Operas and Plays*, p. 40.

39. *The Varieties of Religious Experience* (Longmans, Green, 1902), pp. 347–348. James' chapter on saintliness—which he treats as experience or a psychological disposition—is very interesting in connection with *Four Saints* and Gertrude Stein generally. She owed the book little or nothing—least of all her opinion of Saint Teresa—but such passages as the following coincide wonderfully with the opera: "This auroral openness and uplift gives to all creative ideal levels a bright and caroling quality,

128

it can go naturally with Catholicism and it certainly came naturally to Gertrude Stein. The sentence, "Any one to tease a saint seriously," [40] describe the attitude behind the opera, but the attitude is continuous with sanctity and with "any one."

So that there has to be persistent singing, lateral movement, and popular commonplaces, and gaiety, and sanctity, and the miraculous. The opera keeps all of these going pretty well. As:

One two three four five six seven all good children go to heaven some are good and some are bad one two three four five six seven. Saint Therese in a cart drawn by oxen moving around.[41]

.   .   .   .   .

Saint Therese very nearly half inside and half outside the house and not surrounded.

How do you do. Very well I thank you. And when do you go. I am staying on quite continuously. When is it planned. No more than as often.

The garden inside and outside of the wall.

Saint Therese about to be.

The garden inside and outside outside and inside of the wall.[42]

.   .   .   .   .

If it were possible to kill five thousand chinamen by pressing a button would it be done.

Saint Therese not interested.

---

which is nowhere more marked than where the controlling emotion is religious. 'The true monk,' writes an Italian mystic, 'takes nothing with him but his lyre.'" Pp. 266–267.

40. *Four Saints*, p. 15.
41. p. 24.
42. p. 16.

A pleasure April fool's day a pleasure.
Saint Therese seated.
Not April fool's day a pleasure.
Saint Therese seated.
Not April fool's day a pleasure.
Saint Therese seated.
April fool's day April fool's day as not as pleasure as April fool's day not a pleasure.[43]

The text as it stands is a complete thing, with its own literary music and its own movement in space, but it did do remarkably well set to music and staged. The production was extraordinary apt, in keeping up the motion and visual brilliance of the ballet or vaudeville or circus, indeed in so evidently using apparatus from those forms that the audience after the first few moments of shock felt sufficiently at ease with the kind of show to enjoy it. The music went well with it, being melodious and close to the popular and full of a wit and innocence not unlike Satie. The Negro cast was very right, as the Negro, socially habituated to total exposure and bare existence, does have the quality not of coming from anywhere or of going anywhere but simply of staying there or staying around, which is close enough to the essence of sanctity and certainly of this opera. With such an extravagant variety of elements the production was still internally a marvel of coherence, on the very firm theatrical ground of absolute presence. That she figured this ground to herself as landscape or scenery, that it is philosophically and even religiously and sportively and historically firm, may reassure us about the authenticity of force in this opera—that she knew what she was doing. But for all her acute awareness of where she stood in relation

43. p. 16.

to other formulations of life, her force was an independent poetic force, operating on presence in its own way, but at the very center of real human experience. It made the production of *Four Saints* not only very lively and delightful but so immensely real that one felt that the subject matter, the ideas, even the words, had all been a dream and were now coming true on the stage. Which is what only the greatest theater does, and I do not think it had been done in English since Shakespeare. Probably that is because the English theater after Shakespeare got interested in being true to life at its emptiest or in being about something, but nobody seriously felt that life came true on the stage. Not as it did say in science or money or religion or reason.

I don't think that the later plays and operas of Gertrude Stein get beyond *Four Saints,* but there were some very interesting minor developments which may turn out to be the primitives of more elaborated forms in the future.

Shortly after *Four Saints* she wrote: "A name is a place and a time a noun is once in a while." [44] If a name is a place and a time, the chances are that one can write a play about a name. At any rate Gertrude Stein wrote a very interesting little play called "The Five Georges." It is based on the rather convincing fancy that a person has the character of his name, and if for example not all Georges are alike at least they have very much a quality in common, which for Gertrude Stein came down to something like this: "The Georges whom I have known have been pleasant not uninteresting and finally one and finally more often very well estimated as succeeding intelligibly and not more than is necessary as presidents are useful. They are useful in extremes." [45] The utmost in George was for her George Washington, about whom she wrote "a novel or a play" that was included in her posthumous book *Four in America;* but the

44. *How to Write,* p. 207.
45. *Ibid.,* p. 289.

play "The Five Georges" is a presentation of very slight variations of the character George as embodied in five personages who never meet each other until they are gathered together into a sort of bouquet of Georges at the end. One may say it is a series of variations on the theme of George, or a composition in counterpoint in the key of George. This kind of theater, concerned with names and identity, was of course what Pirandello had been doing, in his *Henry IV* and *Così è se vi pare* and so on. But where Pirandello is discursive and philosophical, Gertrude Stein is lyrical and quite plotless. In "The Five Georges" and in other plays she has taken the simple proper name as a sufficient basis of organization. The great play on this theme has not, to my knowledge, been done yet, but if some Chinaman or some Russian would do it, it would be wonderful. They have naturally, I believe, a strong sense of the word not as a utensil but as a marvelous creature in itself.

Another play of Gertrude Stein's, "Three Sisters Who Are Not Sisters," would have delighted Pirandello. It is a murder melodrama in which the characters know only what the audience knows—even the murderer does not know she is the murderer until she is the only one left alive and so evidently must be. This is, of course, a device for keeping the audience in time with the action, and whatever one makes of these late plays as drama, they do contain an extraordinary number of very good theatrical tricks which will probably be used again.

She invented a special kind of anachronistic play in which historical characters of different periods exist together in the stage time; which in turn may or may not be contemporary with the audience. She used this scheme in her last opera, *The Mother of US All*, where the time was the lifetime of Susan B. Anthony and still involved both John Adams and Virgil Thomson. Such trick time schemes usually involve the actual historical present as the basic term played against a remote past, as with *A Connecticut Yankee,* or a remote future, as with *The Time Machine,* but they do not really get away from progressive history as understood by the 19th century. It has in a way been the mission of the 20th century to destroy progressive history and create a single time in which everything in the past and possibly the future would be simultaneous. Proust and Joyce both did it in their ways and Gertrude Stein did it in her way. This time, which one might call legendary time, is the time of the composition, or rather within the composition, within the Proustian novel, and within *Finnegans Wake.* In the plays of Gertrude Stein of course it is the stage present. She said in *Lucy Church Amiably:* "Supposing everyone lived at the same time what would they say. They would observe that stringing beans is universal." [46] Whereas in the 19th century games with progressive time any item in ordinary experience became absurd when seen in the context of another period, in this legendary time of the 20th century it is possible to see a string bean or a human character or any incident as an absolute existence. The "scientific" time of the 19th century destroyed the validity of present existence, but the created continuous present of Gertrude Stein and others in the 20th century rescues not only present or current existence but even the past by including everything equally within the mind or the work and composing the ingredients on the basis of their immediate qualities, not on the basis of their historical context. The religious equivalent of this time is eternity or simply legend. Something of the same time sense governed Picasso's use of older styles in his painting. It is Spanish, this sense of constant legend as against history, but it is also Greek, and I believe, classical. And there is reason enough to believe that it is perfectly American. In any case the stage is the right place for such a thing—at least the Greek theater and the French theater of the 17th

46. *Lucy Church Amiably,* p. 21.

century made the most of it, and even *A Connecticut Yankee* and *The Sense of the Past* wound up on the stage. And more recently, *Finnegans Wake* found itself happily on the boards as *The Skin of Our Teeth.*

Gertrude Stein did a number of charming things with legend on the stage, but I think her faster and more furious games with time and identity came in other forms—the novel and biography.

5. *The Trouble with Novels*

One of the things that happened at the end of the nineteenth century was that nobody knew the difference between a novel and a play and now the movies have helped them not to know but although there is none there really is and I know there is and that is the reason I write plays and not novels.[1]

. . . . . .

. . . plays are that, they are the thing anybody can see by looking. Other things are what goes on without everybody seeing, that is why novels are not plays well anyway. . . . In America they want to make everything something anybody can see by looking. That is very interesting, that is the reason there are no fences in between no walls to hide anything no curtains to cover anything and the cinema that can make anything be anything anybody can see by looking.[2]

These remarks are worth dwelling on a little, if only because they help to explain the painful situation of the American novel. The traditional novel was based on privacy —"what goes on without everybody seeing"—but the American sense of any effective and interesting existence is largely

1. *Everybody's Autobiography*, p. 194.
2. *Ibid.*, pp. 195–196.

a matter of publicity, so that we have to complicate the pure and simple novel with theatricalism, or the epic, or a jazz lyricism, not to mention writing indirectly for the movies. Admittedly the novel has been from its beginnings a mixed form, and its great virtue has been that almost anything can be done with it, but what the novel depends on as other forms do not is a private and intimate and personal sense of the casual sensations and incidents of everyday life. It lives on gossip, secrecies, matters of taste and tone, an acute sense of conventions and eccentricities and relativities. Which is why it has often been written in letters or as a confession, and can scarcely get along without an adultery or a murder mystery even now. But even if it takes on a big subject, like the Napoleonic wars or the Dreyfus case or the destiny of man, the true novel still treats it privately or as it were confidentially.

The story about "Dr. Livingstone, I presume" is a model of novelistic manner, and the really extraordinary development of the 19th century English novel is largely due to the national necessity of making privacy—as private property, private enterprise, privateering, and private life—equal to the great wide weird world outside the island.[3] It is like the immense domesticity of Queen Victoria, Empress of India. When, by the end of the 19th century, the nation, the class, and the family were no longer adequate shelters or frames for the private vision, the novel was written on the private experience of the completely exposed and sensitized individual, with various attempts to ritualize or authenticate such experience by myth or manner or density of stylistic texture. As with the involutions of the Proustian sentence or the medieval begaudedness of *Ulysses*. The

3. Cf. *Lectures in America*, p. 28: ". . . in the 19th century when the inside had become so solidly inside that all the outside could be outside and still the inside was all inside."

revival of surrealism after its apparent death in 1935 or so is the most recent attempt to save the validity of the novel as private experience. If at the end of the 19th century nobody knew the difference between a novel and a play—largely because of the imperial exhibition of insular privacies like teatime in India—nobody now knows the difference between a novel and lyric poetry. At least Virginia Woolf and D. H. Lawrence never knew.

The question of the American novel is slightly different. Even our traditional novel, since Hawthorne,[4] has been theatrical and without a sound sense of privacy, because we live on a continent where things may get lost but cannot really be concealed, so that interiors have no meaning. So that our current struggle about the individual and the community is quite serious, the individual being in considerable danger of not existing at all. Most countries have been settled long enough on an agrarian and clan basis for the individual to go on and on in perfect reality no matter how the community is exaggerated, but with us the individual can exist only in solitude, which is an entirely different thing from privacy, or in public, and if the public life becomes too full of anonymity and groups and types the individual is thrown back on simple solitude, which has virtually no meaning any more, and certainly not a novelistic one. There is the regional novel and the minority novel and the period novel, but none of these devices I think makes enough of a privacy for the novel to be perfectly real. On the whole the only American novelists who can really work in and extend the tradition of the novel as private vision are the Southerners, especially those from Mississippi, the most exquisitely private state in the Union. But the

4. I mean that in *The Scarlet Letter* and *The House of Seven Gables,* for example, the concealments and secrecies are treated *visually* and *theatrically.*

continental American has to sustain himself on public forms like the theater or the epic, or on a solitary form like the lyric. Or a combination of these, the romance.

Those at any rate are some of the reasons that Gertrude Stein did not write real novels. But more important is the fact that an "impulse for elemental abstractions" leads anywhere but to the novel, which lives by its concrete relativities. For example the Greeks, who had eminently that impulse, got around to the epic, the lyric, and the drama very well but never to the novel. It was even very late before they got to the pastoral romance which is sometimes called the Greek novel. And even the pastoral romance grew out of a half lyrical, half theatrical form invented in extremities by Theocritus. So that it comes quite naturally that what I think is Gertrude Stein's most important novel,[5] *Lucy Church Amiably,* is really a pastoral romance, and very close to lyricism and the theater. It was written in 1927, just after *Four Saints in Three Acts.* The writing was still dominated by melody and landscape, and so the book is a vital rediscovery of the pastoral, a reliving of the inside and outside realities that occasioned the first pastorals, and is not even remotely a literary imitation of the earlier versions. She went back not to literary nature but to nature, and she took it this time not as an accompaniment or illustration to character, as in *Three Lives,* or as the outside reality, as in *Tender Buttons,* or as the world, as in *Four Saints,* but as simply beautiful. After the introduction the book begins with this announcement:

To bring them back to an appreciation of natural beauty or the beauty of nature hills valleys fields and birds. They will say it is beautiful but will they sit in it. This brings us to Lucy Church or Lucy Pagoda preferably Lucy Church.

5. I mean the most important so far in print. The unpublished "Mrs. Reynolds" is probably her masterpiece in this form.

138

This brings to Lucy Church. The beauties of nature hills valleys trees fields and birds. Trees valleys fields flocks and butterflies and pinks and birds. Trees fields hills valleys birds pinks butter-flies clouds and oxen and walls of a part of a building which is up.[6]

That is Theocritean even to the somewhat arch humor, but if she was influenced at all it was probably by the inner temper of these years before 1929 and then by the kind of painting it produced. She had started buying the painting of Francis Rose and looking at the painting of Bérard, Berman, and Tchelitchew. Something vaguely called neoromanticism was on, Gris had gone lyrical, and even Picasso in these years [7] was indulging in agreeable subject matter and quite often in large easy lines as never before.[8] His addiction to sheer calligraphy corresponded quite closely to her addiction to sheer melodiousness. It was the middle of the twenties and there was nothing to make the easy and delicate pleasures of life unconvincing except perhaps to economists and moralists. *Lucy Church Amiably* is advertised both on the cover and the title page as "a novel of romantic beauty and nature and which looks like an engraving" and so was meant to be lovely and pleasurable and not heroic or deep. She said in 1929 that "painting now after its great moment must come back to be a minor art," [9] and she may have felt something of the same thing

6. P. 47. Cf. also "Three Sitting Here" (1927), in *Portraits and Prayers*, p. 124: ". . . the necessity of everybody rejoining lilies of the valley and everything."

7. In 1927 he stopped painting for six months. That time, and the following years, were full of struggle to get back his own vision, which he was tempted to falsify with various sentimentalities. Gertrude Stein's account of the struggle (*Picasso*, pp. 41–42) is very clear.

8. So, in music, was Stravinsky with his *Apollon Musagète*, composed in 1927–1928.

9. *How to Write*, p. 13.

about writing. At least she was convinced that there was a new movement on in both writing and painting, and the new movement in painting was represented by the thoroughly pleasurable and unheroic art of Francis Rose and the neoromantics then. The movement in writing in 1927 may be indicated by assorted works in *transition* which tend to much the same thing—including a reprint of Joyce's "Anna Livia Plurabelle," a translation of part of Gide's *Les Nourritures terrestres,* and actually a *Pastorale* by Jolas. It would be nice to have an inside history of that year, a year so tender that even the great utterance of Vanzetti fairly melts with it.

In 1928 Gertrude Stein announced that "Romance is everything," [10] and in a special sense *Lucy Church Amiably* is a romantic work, as *Tender Buttons* had been in another sense. Neither has anything much to do with the literary tradition of romanticism, for all that Lamartine gets into *Lucy Church Amiably* and his lake is not far away from the landscape described. It is, to start with, a landscape novel, as her recent plays had been landscapes, and it is firmly settled in a spatial here and now. That is unlike historical romanticism, and belongs rather to an immediate sense of romance, an extension of the saintly delight over the present world as expressed in *Four Saints.* The whole attitude of the novel can be summed up in the sentence, "In this and sweetly." [11] The kind of "romance" it contains is clear from the sentence, "Sentiment is awhile and weighed as a weight and romance is made to be authentic." [12] That is, where traditional romantic feeling is concerned with the temporary and so to speak endured by the writer, ·

10. *Useful Knowledge,* advertisement.

11. *Lucy Church Amiably,* p. 26. Cf. in *Four Saints,* p. 33: "In this and in this and in this and clarity." This registers well enough the difference in intensity and quality between the two works.

12. *How to Write,* p. 16.

140

romance is permanent and real and known by the writer. Or, more correctly, it is the romance of the classical predecessors of romanticism, like Goldsmith and Bernardin de Saint-Pierre, and *Lucy Church Amiably* belongs in the company of *The Vicar of Wakefield* and *Paul et Virginie,* ultimately to the vein of *Daphnis and Chloë.* It has their sweetness and their extraordinarily firm and clear reality. But Gertrude Stein said at least as much as all that in saying the book looked like an engraving, and in mentioning illustrations of *Paul et Virginie.*[13]

The theme, or metronome, sentence of *Lucy Church Amiably* may be taken as an example of the quality of the whole book: "Select your song she said and it was done and then she said and it was done with a nod and then she bent her head in the direction of the falling water. Amiably." [14] Most of the passages in the book have the wonderful ease and beauty of that one. Admittedly a great deal of the charm depends on one's conventionally tender feelings about the things mentioned—the book is all over flowers and birds and other natural wonders as announced—and upon the cursive calligraphy, the melodic progress at an adagio tempo. Even this movement is a transcription of a "romantic" reality in the landscape, the movement of clouds and wind and especially water in rain, waterfalls, rivers, and inundations. She was as usual at the very source of her form, here the source of the pastoral, whether musical or literary. She had already trained herself in this kind of transcription of movement, and as she says,[15] ". . . I concentrated the internal melody of existence that I had learned in relation to things seen into the feeling I then [1922] had there in Saint Remy of light and air and air moving and being still. I worked at these things then with a great

13. *Lucy Church Amiably,* p. 81.
14. *Ibid.,* advertisement and p. 19.
15. *Lectures in America,* p. 197.

deal of concentration and as it was to me an entirely new way of doing it I had as a result a very greatly increased melody." Her belief that people are formed by the climate they live in—not merely the temperature but the movement of air and light and water—does not in the least mean that she thought her climatological calligraphy justified by its being true to the place it was written in, it simply means that she took these natural phenomena and their qualities to be an intimately human affair and so a proper articulation of human expression. This is, incidentally, a part of Gertrude Stein's orientalism, that sort of intimate exchange between man and nature that appears in Chinese painting or Hindu sculpture, where the human figure is expressed not in terms of Greek proportions and canonized anatomy but in terms of the movement of streams or vines. In Gertrude Stein's writing at this time, human thoughts and actions follow the movement of natural powers.

Sometimes the transcription of nature is literal, as in:

If there is a river and it is known that it is filled with water and that the water is flowing faster when there is more water it is very easy to see that more water flows into the river and that the water in the river is running along faster very much faster as there is very much more water in the river.[16]

And less literally, the motion of this:

Lucy Church can not complain if he is told if he is told if he is told she can not complain if he is told if he is told if he is told if he is told about it and as he is told about it he knows that he is told about it and he knows that a whole regiment is in some countries four thousand men and in some countries is one thousand men and in some

16. *Lucy Church Amiably,* p. 93.

142

countries is twelve hundred men and in some countries is nine hundred men if he is told about it.[17]

And here is a description of a man living and moving very much as the air or a slight wind or a cloud might move:

He got up and he sat down and he walked around. He came back. He liked it. He was ready to tell her what she should tell him. He hesitated. He was very much obliged. He was as much as you like what is as much as you like. He was called William Mary and he employed Albert Bigelow. As William Mary he lived here. As employing Albert Bigelow he lived here. As getting up sitting down and walking around he lived here.[18]

This kind of movement is absolutely right for the pastoral, and so are the quantities of scenery described. I think it all goes to make the purest and best pastoral romance we have had in this century. But both the material and the method are determined by a sense of natural beauty, and while such a sense can make an exciting work if the natural beauty is just beginning to be discovered or is suddenly rediscovered, it does after a while begin to prejudice experience and the serious creative artist has to rid himself of it. Gertrude Stein "sat" in natural beauty long enough to give us *Lucy Church Amiably* and a few other works, like *An Acquaintance with Description*, but then she had to begin again.

The new beginning took her still farther away from the novel proper, to an incredibly close analysis of grammar and the intellectual movement within sentences, and then to poetry written in almost total independence of the visible world.

17. *Ibid.*, p. 151.
18. *Ibid.*, p. 139.

I began to feel movement to be a different thing than I had felt it to be.

It was to me beginning to be a less detailed thing and at the same time a thing that existed so completely inside in it and it was it was so completely inside that really looking and listening and talking were not a way any longer needed for me to know about this thing about movement being existing.[19]

In writing *Lucy Church Amiably* she had seen everything as a natural phenomenon existing in itself except only for its existence and movement within the landscape, and everything could be brought to exist and move in the book just as it was seen to exist in the landscape. While the stylistic organization of the book is intense and continuous enough to float it,[20] so to speak, as a thing in itself, the composition does reflect or parallel in great detail the intricacies of relation and movement in the real landscape. But now the real existence of the subject matter was to be further isolated, having a relation only to itself and then to the mind of the writer, quite outside of space and time. Movement in space is replaced by vibration or sheer intensity of assertion. This situation led her to the discovery that poetry is based on the noun, on the passionate calling on the name of anything. The simple and intense calling on a name at least makes a completely present act of the essential relationship between the writer and the isolated object. It is the purest possible expression of the act of knowing.

Poetry is I say essentially a vocabulary just as prose is essentially not.

19. *Ibid.*, p. 202.
20. Cf. *ibid.*, p. 169: "Why has no one written the biography of the man who thought of and made the soap that floats. It would be interesting."

*And what is the vocabulary of which poetry absolutely
is. It is a vocabulary entirely based on the noun as prose
is essentially and determinedly and vigorously not based
on the noun.*

*Poetry is concerned with using with abusing, with los-
ing with wanting, with denying with avoiding with re-
placing the noun. It is doing that always doing that, doing
that and doing nothing but that. Poetry is doing nothing
but using losing refusing and pleasing and betraying and
caressing nouns.*[21]

I shall not attempt to describe the later poetry of Gertrude
Stein. She herself said it was very difficult to express what
she meant by it except as she did in the work itself, and
that is the way with any very intense poetry. She wanted
to create, on the basis of the noun, a thing completely
existing in itself, being completely its own movement, and
as it were folded upon or into itself. This poetical absolute
not unnaturally bears a resemblance to various theological
constructions of God as pure Being and unrelated being and
unmoved movement and so on. And in our present paroxysm of mechanics aviation is reaching almost the same
kind of absolute movement and detached, not even self-
related entity. Very likely ski jumping is another physical
expression of the same impulse. Gertrude Stein used a
passage from her portrait of Georges Hugnet to illustrate
what she meant at this point. "It is all there," she said.

*George Genevieve Geronimo straightened it out without
their finding it out.*

*Grammar makes George in our ring which Grammar
makes George in our ring.*

*Grammar is as disappointed not is as grammar is as
disappointed.*

21. *Lectures in America,* p. 231.

145

Grammar is not as Grammar is as disappointed.
George is in our ring. Grammar is not is disappointed. In
are ring.
George Genevieve in are ring.[22]

This is difficult, but the appreciation of it as usual does
not depend upon having information about the subject
matter—who George, Genevieve, and Geronimo were and
what they straightened out—but upon a susceptibility to
the tension or pulsation produced by the incantation of
names, the repetition of names and propositions, by the
contradictions and the transformation produced by a very
slight change of a vowel, from "in our ring" to "in are
ring." [23] It depends on having as acute a rhetorical sense as
that required for reading Ovid or Ronsard, or in the English tradition the sort of thing that is frequent enough in
Shakespeare and Donne:

Thus far for love, my love-suit, sweet, fulfill.
Will will fulfill the treasure of thy love,
Ay, fill it full with wills, and my will one . . .

. . . . .

Let Maps to other, worlds on worlds have shown,
Let us possess one world, each hath one, and is one.

22. *Ibid.*, p. 203.
23. This use of the off-rhyme is independent of the rather
general modern usage of off-rhymes derived from Hopkins and,
through T. S. Eliot and Ezra Pound, from the 13th and 14th
century Italians. One can only say that both usages come ultimately from a *calligraphic* sense of words and ideas. The vogue
for Dante is due mainly to our revived sense of such calligraphy,
but behind Dante are Byzantium and Arabia, the Orient. St.
Thomas and the Provençal poets were perfectly calligraphical and
did not, in this respect, deorientalize things for Dante. I do not
know why the 20th century should be at home with calligraphy,
but it is worth observing that the dominant science of the 20th
century is physics, as against the biology of the 19th and the
146

One has been taught to deplore this kind of thing wherever it comes, as one is told not to like puns or rhyming in prose, but it happens all the time that the intellect in its most intense relationship with its object and in trying to make the calling of the name adequate and concentrated and exact has recourse to these repetitions and involutions, which maintain the presence of the object more intensely than the similar devices of metaphor and discourse. At any rate the degree of intensity and reduction Gertrude Stein was after in that passage may be imagined from her comment, ". . . all that was necessary was that there was something completely contained within itself and being contained within itself was moving, not moving in relation to anything not moving in relation to itself but just moving, I think I almost at that time did this thing." [24] This terrific attempt to express a concentrated knowing of a living thing while foregoing discourse and melody and movement in space may, while perfectly intellectual in intention and method and not mystic, be compared to the exquisite isolated energy, the ecstasy of Plotinus' mind approaching the vision of God. Gertrude Stein was capable of quite simply staring into the sun, and at this point she seems to have had intellectually the same almost blinding vision of anything alive. I regret very much having no closer an understanding of her work at that time than that, but it is enough for tracing the general logic of her later work to know that at this time her mind had been strenuously and almost suicidally alone with its object, that she had approached a kind of intellectual eternity, and when she came away from that position it was to problems determined by it, that is, the problems of time and identity and exactly what is the

geometry of the 17th and 18th, and *stylistically* speaking, physics is calligraphic, not structural like geometry, or, like biology, concerned with modulations of growth.

24. *Lectures in America*, p. 202.

human mind. The skill and penetration and the general ease with which she treated these problems were largely a result of her much more intense and difficult experience of isolated living entities.

This last tired her, she said, and largely to amuse herself she wrote *The Autobiography of Alice B. Toklas* in 1932. The book, in this like Proust, is an attempt to give the past a really present and objective existence. Proust tells about "recapturing" the past by way of actual physical sensations, but his actual re-creation of the past is the writing itself, the making it a new discovery as he wrote and an objective thing, a thing exterior to himself. Hence we have that awkward fuss about who the Marcel in the book is, whether he is Proust or a mask or what. He was created distinct from the author at any rate as a sort of backboard or sounding board to send back the past experiences wished on him, send them leaping into a detached and objective and quite new life in the moment of writing. Albeit the more effective isolation of himself from his past life was contrived by Proust in his cork room. Gertrude Stein hit on a much simpler, and for the specific literary purpose of making the past come true and new in the present writing, a more effective device, using as a sounding board her companion Miss Toklas who had been with her for twenty-five years. It has been said that the writing takes on very much Miss Toklas' conversational style,[25] and while this is true the style is still a variant of Miss Stein's conversational style, for she had about the same way with an anecdote or a sly observation in talking as Miss Toklas has. She usually insisted that writing is an entirely different thing from talking, and it is part of the miracle of this little scheme of objectification that she could by way of imitating Miss Toklas put in writing something of her own beautiful con-

25. Carl Van Vechten, in his introduction to *Selected Writings,* pp. xii–xiii.

148

versation. So that, aside from making a real present of her past, she re-created herself, or rather she created a figure of herself, established an identity, a twin, a Doppelgänger who burst into publicity at once and became something not far short of a Frankenstein monster, though a very pretty one indeed. In writing an autobiography she had evidently not written a novel, if the novel is based on what not everybody can see. The book is full of the most lucid and shapely anecdotes, told in a purer and more closely fitting prose, to my sense, than even Gide or Hemingway have ever commanded,[26] but it is based on the long discipline of French conversation which is to an extraordinary degree a matter of general ideas. The most private French life is completely saturated with general ideas, with what is known as *la raison,* so that from the point of view of the English novel almost all French novels have too high a glaze to be at all likable, too much good sense to make good gossip. Proust is an exception, but after all he trained himself on Ruskin and George Eliot. In short French life is more theatrical than novelistic, always more public than private. The frankness and decisiveness and the relative immodesty of the Gallic spirit are part of this. To say nothing of the French sense of fashion, which is all subtlety and nuance and the utmost in sensibility applied to a public presentation. The *Autobiography* has all of this, including the sense of fashion, but even more fatal to the novelistic possibilities is Gertrude Stein's having been for some time determined to be as commonplace as possible.[27] Such an intention belongs to the classical artist doing an epic, a play, or a lyric, but it certainly is no way to write a novel, not even a naturalistic or proletarian novel. Leo Stein called

26. She said she meant to write the book as simply as Defoe wrote the autobiography of Robinson Crusoe, and Defoe's absolute rational and commonplace clarity may have influenced her style somewhat.

27. *The Autobiography of Alice B. Toklas,* pp. 185–186.

149

the book a romance—in quite another sense, of course [28]—
but it is a romance.

However, Gertrude Stein did in this work return to narrative, and the possibilities of narrative, the question of
its reality, became the great occupation of the rest of her
life, so much so that when she had read aloud her last
book, *Brewsie and Willie,* she declared that what she
had after all done in writing was for narrative. I think she
did a great deal more than what she did for narrative,
but certainly her clarification of narrative is very important.

She came at it something like this. If, as in the poetry I
very loosely described a few pages back, the object is conceived as a disembodied movement, free of space and
contained within itself, and simply present to the mind, it
is essentially an event.[29] It may be conceived not as a result or as the beginning of other consequences but purely
and simply as a present happening. And that can be taken
as the final reality, since causalities are induced by action
and reflection. Gertrude Stein's previous suppression of
causalities had resulted in present existence as the final reality, a reality that could be expressed in terms of a continuous
present and participles, as in *The Making of Americans,* or in
terms of space, as in *Tender Buttons* and the "middle writ-

28. I cannot of course judge, as a witness of the events, the ve-
racity of the book, and it is nothing to my purpose, but for example Arnold Rönnebeck checked her account of conversations
against his account of them written down in his notebooks the
same day they took place, and the two accounts were nearly identical. He decided she must have kept notebooks too—the conversations being of 1912—but she did not. She only had an extraordinary verbal memory and, there is every reason to believe,
a perfectly simple honesty.

29. This coincides, I believe accidentally, with her friend
Whitehead's use of the word "event" to mean what is usually referred to as an object. The coincidence with Valéry's *évènement
pur* is also just a coincidence.

ing" which was really painting. But if the final reality is not existence or Being but pure present eventuality, everything in writing comes into question again. Philosophically it is hard to know what you really mean by Being, but if it is understood to be a permanent state and a finality—as against process and becoming—one does wish, for the sake of a complete and immediate conception or possession of reality, to get Being and eventuality together at once, by equating them or absorbing one in the other. So in religion we get all eventuality conceived at once in the divine mind and so on. The literary problem is of course rather different, but it can reasonably be taken as the effort to conceive and express sheer happening so intensely that it becomes complete in itself, that it has final being. Or to deal with anything as if its arrival in the here and now, in the moment of writing, were the essence of it. Gertrude Stein analyzed the difficulty of newspaper writing for example as the suicidal attempt to make the events of yesterday real tomorrow, so that the event is never real in the present of writing.[30] It is also the problem of the historian who cannot get the events he writes about to exist and be in the present of his writing. What Gertrude Stein did with the historian's problem I shall describe shortly. But the novelist's problem is that he cannot seriously believe any longer in the finality of sheer eventfulness. He uses events to reveal character or to provoke the emotions of real action, but essentially for the disturbances and vibrations they set up in the enclosure of the private life. The only major works I know of which take mere and sheer external eventfulness as the absolute and sufficient reality are the *Iliad* and *The Arabian Nights*, both of them products of the Orient. If one includes the picaresque novel, as *Lazarillo de Tormes* or as *Gil Blas*, and in the theater Corneille and Calderón, one is still not out of the Orient because one is in

30. *Narration* (University of Chicago Press, 1935), pp. 35–37.

Spain.[31] At all events the assumption of sheer eventfulness as a finality is natural in the Orient, where its counterpoise, fatalism, is natural, and Gertrude Stein was perfectly conscious of having her part in the present orientalization of the West.[32] Her rediscovery of pure narrative is really part of it. Her narrative was not, not even in *The Autobiography of Alice B. Toklas*, a matter only of external events. The full sense of eventfulness inevitably includes what happens in thinking or looking or listening or talking or feeling as well as what happens in things being physically done. But the outside or inside historical event can at the most be understood as a sort of dress rehearsal for the real event, which is the written event. "Vasari and Plutarch . . . make them up so completely that if they are not invented, they might as well be they do not really feel that any one of the ones about whom they tell had any life except the life they are given by their telling." [33] Also the Homer of the *Iliad*, and Herodotus, and even Thucydides had the same feeling, but as soon as history limits itself to being a faithful or instructive account of the facts it is no longer literature. Now precisely this is the problem of autobiography, that it is next to impossible for a writer to feel that his life has not existed except as he writes it, but the scheme of *The Autobiography of Alice B.*

31. In music we get absolute eventfulness in Scarlatti and very much in Mozart. Scarlatti is close enough to the Orient, by Spain and perhaps Naples. The externals of Mozart's orientalism are not so definite. In American writing the kind of thing I mean comes at its clearest perhaps in Dashiell Hammett, who is the Scarlatti of the crime story, with San Francisco his Naples. His plots are not really dramatic or progressive but, like those of Henry James, mere frames for continuous and complete happening, in this case of course mainly external happening. It was no doubt this absolutism of eventfulness that Gertrude Stein admired in Hammett.

32. *Everybody's Autobiography*, pp. 10, 21, 22.

33. *Narration*, p. 61.

Toklas does allow it to happen—Gertrude Stein's life as reflected by Miss Toklas can be created as a new thing by Gertrude Stein writing. The scheme of the second autobiography, *Everybody's Autobiography,* is an extension of the first. Having created her twin or reflection in the first autobiography and committed it to the public, she had to watch this second "Gertrude Stein" get entirely away from her, as it was elaborated upon by the enormous publicity it received during her tour of America in 1934–35. So that now she could discover her past and present as reflected by "everybody" just as before they had been reflected by Miss Toklas. Discovering that even her childhood now belonged to the celebrity "Gertrude Stein" she could write about "herself" endlessly enough, and it has been very well said that she became her own Boswell.[34] She often said that the essence of being a genius was the ability to talk and listen at the same time, and being her own Boswell certainly reinforced that situation. Whatever one feels about this elaboration of egoism, the curious result is that in *Everybody's Autobiography,* in *Wars I Have Seen,* and in *Paris France* there is a sort of "aesthetic distance" created by which the endless talk about herself and her writing and her opinions and the little incidents that happened to her all seems objective and final and complete on the page and does not worry the reader with the feeling of being confided in or impressed personally by the writer. The technique of autobiographical novels, which use "he" or "she" instead of "I" to avoid this embarrassment of seeming to climb into the reader's lap, is reversed in these books where "Gertrude Stein" is really a third person speaking in the first—as when Johnson is quoted by Boswell. Or, if you like, it is an actor's technique, and in any case it is part of an enormously public performance. But meanwhile the

34. By Robert B. Haas, in his introduction to *What Are Masterpieces* (Conference Press, 1940), p. 14.

natural question arose, who and what is Gertrude Stein, if all the personal history, the ideas and feelings and incidents and public importance all belong to "Gertrude Stein?" The answer gradually became that the residual Gertrude Stein was an otherwise anonymous force of existence, or mind, or genius, but the ironies of the undefined situation were beautifully exploited in a series of works on "Identity" and in particular in the novel called *Ida*.

Ida is strictly speaking no novel at all but belongs to the tradition of the philosophical farce or romance which is probably at its purest in Voltaire's *Candide*. In a vague way *Ida* is about the Duchess of Windsor, but it is really the story of what Gertrude Stein called a "publicity saint," that is a person who neither does anything nor is connected with anything but who by sheer force of existence in being there holds the public attention and becomes a legend. It is quite like what we mean by saying a person is a name. Or it is like the heroines of old romances who simply exist, or the faraway princesses of the romantics who do nothing and have no personalities but just exist. Or it is like the women on the society page of newspapers, or the really great movie stars who do not have to act but are simply there, which is enough. Ida is a sort of combination of Helen of Troy, Dulcinea, Garbo, the Duchess of Windsor, and in particular "Gertrude Stein." The extraordinary thing about the book is that it manages to maintain a level and atmosphere of legend, this legend being a fascinating mixture of Homer and Hollywood and the daily press.

Ida woke up. After a while she got up. Then she stood up. Then she ate something. After that she sat down.
  That was Ida.[35]

. . . . .

35. *Ida* (Random House, 1941), p. 55.

Ida never sighed, she just rested. When she rested she turned a little and she said, yes dear. She said that very pleasantly.

This was all of Ida's life just then.[36]

. . . . . .

It is difficult never to have been younger but Ida almost was she almost never had been younger.[37]

. . . . .

Ida never spoke, she just said what she pleased. Dear Ida.[38]

. . . . . .

Ida moved around, to dance is to move around to move around is to dance, and when Ida moved around she let her arms hang out easily in front of her just like that.[39]

. . . . .

Once upon a time there was a city, it was built of blocks and every block had a square in it and every square had a statue and every statue had a hat and every hat was off.

Where was Ida where was Ida.

She was there. She was in Washington and she said thank you very much, thank you very much indeed. Ida was in Washington.[40]

This last passage, the description of Washington with Ida in it, while externally inaccurate, in internally true, by using on that charming and quite legendary city a manner that might belong to a description of Bagdad in *The Arabian*

36. p. 34.
37. p. 114.
38. p. 130.
39. p. 72.
40. p. 73.

Nights. One can introduce either with the formula "Once upon a time," and it is right, for though the city is still there it is a legend. And in that has much the same kind of existence as Ida. The book treats states like Ohio and Texas and Montana and other cities in much the same way. There is the old joke about Boston not being a city but a state of mind, and that reality is applied carefully to the descriptions not only of Boston but to most of our geography. One result of all this is that the stylistic texture of the book closely resembles a Persian miniature, as *Lucy Church Amiably* looked like an engraving. For example in actual physical descriptions:

Once upon a time there was a shotgun and there were wooden guinea hens and they moved around electrically, electricity made them move around and as they moved around if you shot them their heads fell off them.[41]

One day in Texas it was not an accident, believe it or not, a lizard did sit there. It was almost black all over and curled, with yellow under and over, hard to tell, it was so curled, but probably under.[42]

Or in the handling of a little episode:

Ida was married and they went to live in Ohio. She did not love anybody in Ohio.

She liked apples. She was disappointed but she did not sigh. She got sunburned and she had a smile on her face. They asked her did she like it. She smiled gently and left it alone. When they asked her again she said not at all. Later on when they asked her did she like it she said. Perhaps only not yet.

Ida left Ohio.[43]

41. p. 61.
42. p. 56.
43. p. 51.

156

And then in the long interpolated section on all the dogs Ida has known in her life, and the very pretty sort of prose *guignol* involving the personnel of superstitions—spiders, dwarfs, cuckoos, and goldfish—the same so to speak Persian quality is maintained—the quiet, the brilliance, the elegance, the simplicity and the even interest of detail, but particularly the special legendary reality. I said *Ida* was like *Candide,* and it is, and Voltaire also fancied the Oriental tale. Why Western intellect in a vein of elegance and unreality takes so readily to Persia I do not quite know, but I think it is not only a fact but a future. Still, though Gertrude Stein was often aware of orientalizing, the specific qualities of *Ida* are probably derived not from Persia but from the personality of the Duchess of Windsor as a publicity figure, and if Gertrude Stein thought of any moguls at all it was probably those of the movies. But Persia makes an excellent tuning fork, if not for the writing, certainly for the reading of Ida.

But to come back to the "thesis" of *Ida.* One can take the thesis or leave it alone, as one can the thesis of *Candide,* but *Ida* is by its thesis an existentialist masterpiece, and that may have some importance. No character was ever more "contingent" than Ida, not even in Kafka, and much of the book is an account of her search for her essence, for self-realization. She is a subject in search of a predicate, or an x in search of an equation. She is, it is true, born with a twin—as Ida-Ida—but by the time she is in adolescence the twin or the identity has somehow disappeared and has to be reinvented. The twin comes true when Ida wins a beauty contest. "Nobody knew anything about her except that she was Ida but that was enough because she was Ida the beauty Ida." [44] But when Ida is identified to herself she renames the twin or publicity projection Winnie, because she is always winning, and gradually Winnie

44. p. 20.

disappears. Ida is now perfectly self-contained, she is just an entity, though she wanders about having various functions and dogs and husbands and being always very well known. It is now the predicates which become contingent, simply witnesses to Ida's complete entity. In existentialist terms, her simple existence has become her essence.

Ida decided that she was just going to talk to herself. Anybody could stand around and listen but as for her she was just going to talk to herself.

She no longer even needed a twin.[45]

The effect of one of her most intimate witnesses, a husband named Andrew, is only to make her more herself:

And now Ida was not only Ida she was Andrew's Ida and being Andrew's Ida Ida was more that Ida she was Ida itself.[46]

For a while "it was not so important that Ida was Ida," [47] but finally:

What happened was this.

Ida returned more and more to be Ida. She even said she was Ida.

What, they said. Yes, she said. And they said why do you say yes. Well she said I say yes because I am Ida.

It got quite exciting.[48]

All these vicissitudes of Ida's identity are normal enough in any life, but as Gertrude Stein observed in *The Geographical History of America,* "nobody has identity. Do they put up with it. Yes they put up with it. They put up

45. p. 43.
46. p. 90.
47. p. 94.
48. p. 146.

with identity." [49] At least Ida does, in her later phases, because her present entity is so complete that she does not, as a great many people think they do, require identity to relieve or support or realize or destroy their simple present entities. Ida, and this is the heart of the thesis and the sharpest irony of the book, is a human mind. She has no personality, as Gertrude Stein had declared in the *Geographical History* that personality has nothing to do with the human mind. [50] She had relegated time and identity and personality to human or animal nature, and Ida is really free from all of that. The difference between men and animals is, we are told, that men can count, and Ida can count beautifully up to ten again and again and everybody listens. In the human mind there is neither beginning nor ending, and when Ida finally reaches her sanctity "she did not catch up with anything and did not interrupt anything and did not begin anything and did not stop anything." [51] In short she exists and is in the present, like a legend or a masterpiece or the human mind, and that existence is all there is to her, though she is surrounded by everything else in perpetual happening. [52] Any little hap-

49. *Geographical History*, p. 207.
50. *Ibid.*, p. 143.
51. pp. 150–151.
52. p. 139. "So much happened but nothing happened to Ida. To have anything happen you have to choose and Ida never chose." This is an infrequent position in Gertrude Stein's thinking. Normally the human mind is taken to be perpetual choice—which would result in writing as perpetual happening. But here, as in some other passages, the mind is just there as things happen. As an inert fatality it is the counterpoise to happening, giving happening its reality, witnessing and describing it. The mind may be considered as not even choosing to be there, as being put and kept there by a separate force. Gertrude Stein could say such things, as experience does frequently look like that, but whatever or whoever it is that makes the choices in looking and writing and doing, whether the choices are no more than a sensitive response to newly manifested necessities rather than to past ones, some-

159

pening, however, takes on the force of a miracle or a sign or a portent in happening near Ida, and she is accompanied by other walking legends like army officers and politicians, the unemployed and people who have a stroke of luck or a destiny or a specialty. Ida has more than her share of "daily miracles." Now the philosophical question of how the human mind exists and is by sheer presence, in perfectly inconsequential cognition, is currently amusing, as the question of optimism was amusing in Voltaire, but from the point of view of literature such questions have to be treated as mere aids or occasions for the literary event, and *Ida* is a big event in the question of narrative. Narrative cannot possibly go on living by its truth to the historical facts or to the psychological or moral facts, or by having one thing lead to another; it has now to go on the conviction that sheer happening in the immediate present, and above all in the immediate written present, is the final reality. In short the business of the narrative artist is now, as it was with Homer and Shahrazad, the creation of legend.

One of the strange things about legend is that in it the difference between privacy and publicity, between subjectivity and objectivity, is really destroyed, or they are made continuous on the plane of sheer happening. There is no subjectivity or objectivity in the life of Achilles or of Little Red Riding Hood. And in America: "Once upon a time way back there were always gates, gates that opened

_____

thing in Gertrude Stein maintained this choosing at a greater intensity and frequency than anyone else of her time in writing. The principles of disconnection, abstraction, isolation, as well as composition and counting depend on choice or selection. This may be viewed as a necessary or as an arbitrary choice, but the choice is there, even if it is caused by the impulse or necessity of being fully present to what is newly there, chosen out of what has been there. This is one of the problems, of course, that is always lived in but never solved. Gertrude Stein normally lived in it as if presence and choice were gratuitous, that is—complete within the moment of writing.

160

so that you could go in and then little by little there were no fences or walls anywhere. For a little time they had a gate even when there was no fence. It was just there to look elegant and it was nice to have a gate that would click even if there was no fence. By and by there was no gate." [53]

So that the American thing has become a wandering about with no sense of inside or outside, which is of course very hard on human nature and creates some very fancy neuroses, but it is also a good preliminary ground for the creation of legend. In the *Iliad* what disposed of inside and outside and sustained legend was the continuous manifestation of natural powers, barely distinguished as human, animal, and divine. And then for a long time the conception of sheer prowess and exploit before the world, adventures and discoveries, made legend. In the case of *The Arabian Nights* it is the constant faith that everything is immediately possible and present to Allah. In America anything that stands or moves by itself and serves no purpose can be a legend, because any such thing is perfectly complete to the simple present attention of the human mind. Gertrude Stein had great hopes for the human mind in America. At any rate an example of American legend on this basis is George Washington standing up in the boat crossing the Delaware or praying at Valley Forge. Or Whistler's mother or the Lone Ranger, or the gold standard, or unconditional surrender, or the battleship *Maine*. The source of all these things is of course in history, but they exist as legend.

Gertrude Stein had already worked passionately on that problem, of the relation of history to legend, or how to make absolute and self-contained literature out of historical material. Plutarch and other ancient historians had quite naturally and mysteriously created literature and legend out of history, even when what they said was true. But

53. p. 30.

now that the historian knows too many interrelated facts about past events he cannot really extricate anything from that past reality enough to believe its real meaning is on his page, so that Gertrude Stein thought the only solution for the historian was to amuse himself with games in his writing. She wrote *Four in America*, using figures who were already legendary or nearly legendary—Grant, Henry James, the Wright brothers, and George Washington—and while keeping their specific quality of mind and personality as they exist in legend, provided them with different careers, making Grant a religious leader, Henry James a general, Wright a painter, and Washington a novelist. Where Plutarch wrote his parallel lives describing heroes in the same career, these parallel lives of Gertrude Stein describe the same hero in a different career. The happenings in the book are however for the most part ideas occurring to Gertrude Stein about exactly what kind of religion Grant would have founded, what sort of battles Henry James would have conducted, and so on. These careers presented as stories, full of incidents and invented famous remarks, might well have been more amusing, but the work then would have been a historical fantasy, rather like *A Connecticut Yankee*, which Gertrude Stein thought was very interesting but not really interesting enough.[54] Such a work would have been only a long paradox played against remembered history, not an elaboration or re-creation of present legend. *Four in America* is thus a group of prolonged meditations on or dwellings on the quality of existence of four legends created by America. The legends are seen against constant existences [55]—American religion and

54. *Narration*, p. 62.

55. In her Spanish period she had done not only portraits but biography (e.g.,"I Must Try to Write the History of Belmonte") by presenting the subject (or in the case of Belmonte the absence of the subject) in the thick of the other objects incidents and impressions present to her with the subject, as the subject actually

landscape, war, painting, literature, and in the case of George Washington, scenery—but the real presence is created by the successive moments of realization or recognition by the writer's mind. And that mind is so preoccupied with "elemental abstractions," which are in a way the legends of thinking, that the work has a continuous and coherent reality, and after so long a time a freshness and beauty in historiography. We are, or we should be, by now, so weary of philosophized history, or mythologized history, and imperative history and all the extenuations of Hegel that any innovation is welcome, and this may well be the beginning of a new method with a long future.[56]

However, I believe that she had greater success and a more complete realization in describing contemporary legends—individual groups and nations—where her direct vision could operate without any preliminary contrivance for putting the past in its place. And she was never in any danger of treating such subjects as contemporary history, of writing documentaries or journalism, both because she knew that Picasso and Paris France and the GI's were not historical facts but legends and because her affections were deeply involved with all of them. So that what she wrote about them was literature.

She could have had no trouble in writing her work on Picasso, even though she wrote it in French. She had been one of the first to discover Picasso as a legend and as the creator of the visual legends of the 20th century, and so to some degree he was her legend. The book is a wonder of complete and ample realization. While in perfect command of all the personal history and the aesthetical argumentation that accompanied the creation of the Picasso

exists in anyone's experience. In the later work "looking and listening" have been abandoned and the context of the subject as experienced is of ideas.

56. Thornton Wilder has already used it in *The Ides of March.*

163

legend, she gives only the essence of his person, as he himself in painting her portrait had given only the essence of Gertrude Stein, and she manages to convey the quality of his paintings as real and exciting experiences, without poetizing them and without a great fuss of critical explanation or justification. He and his paintings exist as legend without all that, and she had the good sense not to try to confuse a legend. I trust I am not confusing hers, but if I am it is not very serious, because it is the essence of legend to survive any amount of true or false enthusiasm or explanation.

Her description of Paris France is full of the same discretion. Not only has France always turned out legends with extraordinary facility and conviction, but she has been herself a legend, to the French people as much as to foreigners, and never more so than when she is at war, whether she wins or loses. She has her moments of indulging in restorations and history but essentially it is the real immediate present that is lived as a legend in France. Hence fashion and so on. But war as it is fought, not as it is historically remembered and accounted for, is intensely legendary, and everyone who is really in it has to behave like a legend. This is why war novels are so difficult to write and read; the private sensibilities and the biographical individual have next to nothing to do with it. Tolstoi could write a novel on war by perfectly understanding the drama of that irrelevance, but most novels reduce war to the private life and torture of the individuals and the moral issue and so simply do not cover enough ground and unhappily they fail to be tragic. At all events France at the beginning of the war was her legendary self with terrible intensity and simplicity, and Gertrude Stein wrote *Paris France* just then. It is, like the *Picasso*, affectionate and full, simple and penetrating. As a matter of historiography it is very interesting because it is a rediscovery of the kind of thing Herodotus did, the portrait of a nation as the land and the people but above all as an actual legend. Herodotus was an Oriental Greek, which furthers the resemblance, and the style of *Paris France* is very like Herodotus, there is the same simple and elegant and wandering and eventful way of making a sentence.

The book which describes the fall of France, the occupation and the liberation, *Wars I Have Seen,* is not so beautiful, but in its way it is more exciting, as the account of the persistence of the French legendary realities through the catastrophe and the long furious and exhausting struggle. It was partly in the demonstration of what she said was the French belief, that life should not be too easy and that, like the phoenix, they must rise again from the ashes, which of course requires being reduced to ashes. Furthermore she recognized that life in those years had reverted to the Middle Ages, full of desperation and chivalry, total insecurity and bursts of glory. It had become a Shakespearean sort of reality, with prophecies constantly coming true in reverse and with more than enough sound and fury and absence of meaning. She has been accused of not understanding the war and of a lack of human sympathy for the French, largely because she had no sentimentality and had too urgent a sense of life and the necessity of present legend to be distracted by simplified moralities or panicky emotionalism. It is true that she had for a while been misled by the prefabricated legends of Spanish fascism and she was probably as confused as anyone by the legend of Pétain, but these errors are due to a too great appetite for life and style, a too vivid sense of immediate reality, not to the indifferent intellectualism for which she is often blamed. Her fondness for books of prophecy during the occupation is part of the same sense—they were far closer to the actual quality of life, closer to the medieval reality of those years than say a coherent book on political economy or a book full of 19th

165

century liberalism. The books of prophecy were perfectly coherent with the legend being lived at that time. It is possible now to look back at the events and be reasonable, to piece out a pseudoscientific and absolutely moral account of what happened, or write a smoothly consecutive and likely story about it, but it was not so. As lived and as legend it was like *Wars I Have Seen*.

Her last book, *Brewsie and Willie*, had much the same difficulties with the moral and patriotic predilections of the public. It describes with astonishing accuracy the legend of the GI as it was being lived and created in Europe at the end of 1944 and the first half of 1945. It was an authentic legend, as real as the embattled farmers or the *grognards* of Napoleon or the doughboy of the first World War, with a definite and recognizable "flavor" or quality or state of mind. It did not go on being lived long, and the story of the dissolution of that legend as an actuality would be very depressing and very interesting. But here suffice it to say that the individual soldiers gradually recovered their private personalities, they became local boys again. In many cases it was not so harmless, and even more sinister legends than that of the petty racketeer threatened to become articulate, but that is another story. While the GI legend was really on, in Paris, it was as *Brewsie and Willie* describes it. The book does not at all describe what individual soldiers privately felt and thought about the war and the world at that time, but it completely expresses the quality of thinking and feeling and behaving that all the individuals together created and more or less insisted on and realized as the GI thing. The legend was not a discipline or a code or a dream of heroism, it was not at all rigid and it certainly allowed for the creation of individual legends or "characters" or variations within the range of the key signature, but that key was determined not by any individual personality, it was set by the group which was American and

166

of the time. The book is a kind of quartet or sextet composed exactly in that key. At least it sounds exact to me, and I was in and out of Paris and Germany at the time, being as GI as possible.

The book is, of course, a political tract as violent as *Uncle Tom's Cabin,* this time against not agrarian and racial but industrial and mental slavery. This immediate moral and historical content is passionately felt and thought and eloquently presented,[57] but except for the little epilogue in which the writer speaks to America in her own person, that content is perfectly enclosed in and subordinated to the literary form which embodies the quality of the GI legend.

The form is roughly a wayward series of conversations which get going and mill along and get interrupted and taken up again among some army men and women in Paris. It has the loose-jointedness and irregular tempo and the funny inconsequential magniloquence that such conversations really had, the kidding and the passionate protest and the passionate conviction as often as not. The ideas are thus conducted on the basis of an inner vital interest and impulse, on a dramatic basis, if you like, rather than an orderly logical one. Which makes *Brewsie and Willie* a remarkable variant of the Platonic dialogue. Plato as an Athenian had a sportive interest in ideas as dramatic events, and would spin out a logical argument with as keen a sense of sheer eventfulness as Mozart or Marivaux in spinning out themes. Not so much as a philosopher but as a literary artist and dramatist, Plato was rococo—the brother of Marivaux under the subject matter—whereas *Brewsie and Willie* is the same sort of thing but in jazz, breaking up the logical melody, the logical beat, according to an organic impulse.

57. Her pitch of feeling in this and most matters may be gathered from her last opera, *The Mother of Us All,* in which both the title and the heroine, Susan B. Anthony, are equivalent to Gertrude Stein.

The Socrates of the piece, "that Stein woman," is mentioned but not present, because after all this book is a record of the GI legend and not the Stein legend. It is at least a very great pleasure to have the philosophical dialogue back again, as a natural development and not as a literary reminiscence. The book is, of course, so little a novel that she didn't even call it one, but she did consider it a success of "narration as the 20th century sees it." [58] It is a narrative of what everybody can see, that is it is basically a theatrical form, and in this case it is a narrative of ideas, in a time that is not historical but legendary, all of which brings us, for all the obvious differences, to the Platonic dialogue. At the end of the first World War the *Socrate* of Erik Satie had appeared—being a "symphonic drama" or a setting of certain passages from the Platonic dialogues in translation [59]—and Gertrude Stein was very fond of it, though I doubt that it even crossed her mind while she was writing *Brewsie and Willie*. It so happens that Satie too was much occupied with legend—Rosicrucian, Rabelaisian, bureaucratic, and Catholic as well as Greek—and so he was good company for Cocteau and the surrealists and dadaists of that postwar; but that he should have taken specifically to the Platonic dialogue at that time as Gertrude Stein did at a similar time probably means that Plato—though not the Platonic "system"—is very close to the reality of the 20th century especially as clarified by war. That reality being unreal and inconsequent and hence pervious to the most unlikely and sportive arrangements by the human mind. Gertrude Stein knew no Greek and believed that Greek literature was of no use

58. Quoted by W. G. Rogers in *When This You See Remember Me*, pp. 237–238.

59. It is interesting that one of the passages is that from the *Symposium* in which Alcibiades compares the conversation of Socrates to the flute playing of Marsyas, provoking the same exhilaration.

whatever to Americans,[60] but I find her running into Greeks at every corner. She was bound to meet them, sharing as she did their passion for elemental abstractions, their enterprise in creating and arranging them, and especially their radical intellectual gaiety. She had their astonishing combination of wisdom and innocence which made the Egyptians say the Greeks were always children and which made of Herodotus, as they say, a writer for philosophers and children.

Her particular narrative for children and philosophers is *The World Is Round.*[61] It is the story, in a mixture of prose and poetry, of a little girl named Rose who climbs up a nameless mountain with a hard blue garden chair in which she will not sit until she has reached the summit. After a number of natural adventures and terrors and temptations on the way, she reaches the summit and sits and sings, but she is all alone and as night begins to fall she gets frightened, in particular because while she knows she is there where she wanted to be she cannot tell where *there* is. Suddenly the place is illuminated by the beams of a revolving searchlight run by her cousin Willie who is on another farther hill, so she is comforted and cries. That is the end, except that they turn out not to be cousins and get married and live happily ever after. One might say it is not a story but *the* story, the everlasting account of the quest or the pilgrimage or the progress of the soul that governs most folklore and legend and children's stories as well as most serious narrative literature and popular fiction. The book is as commonplace and as universal as that, and on the level of the children's story it is brilliantly and amiably handled, completely within the interest of children. It very sternly excludes fairies and the devil and, with

60. Cf. *The Autobiography of Alice B. Toklas,* p. 126.
61. William R. Scott, 1939.

the exception of the charming symbolical scene where people get human natures in the form of wild animals in boats and Willie gets Billie the lion, the story takes the real as the marvelous, as a child does, and assumes that the world is strange enough just in being round. On this basis the child's vision and that of Gertrude Stein are continuous. She can write it without being instructive or patronizing, sentimental or cute. She was used to children and got along with them very well, particularly with French children, who are tough little entities and stand for no nonsense. It is really a children's book.

All the same, Rose and the ascent of the nameless mountain are Gertrude Stein and the progress of her writing, or again they are any saint or artist and his quest for the new and complete vision. When she arrives at the summit and sits down she says, I think. This is, for Gertrude Stein, the central and final reality. She draws no conclusions about her existence as Descartes did with his "cogito ergo sum," and she does not make a tragic dignity of it as Pascal did with his "roseau pensant." Technically one can very well ask what she meant by "I" and what she meant by "think," and she would probably have answered that "I" is only the subject or locale of that verb and that "think" is only the present act of consciousness, and one can carry the argument on endlessly, but "I think" is the last experiential reality, and Gertrude Stein takes it as a thing in itself, without logical or religious consequences, it merely is or happens. Rose's determination to be Rose, her realization of her identity, comes a little later as the darkness grows, but it does not at all follow on "I think." This resumption of the identity after the moment of vision of the Absolute or God or anything taken as a thing in itself is a standard part of the human story. "Man is man was man will be solitary and gregarious," Gertrude Stein said in another book,[62] and

62. *Geographical History*, p. 19.
170

"I think" is the end of solitude just as identity is the end of gregariousness, and Rose and Gertrude Stein and anybody are all torn between the two.

The human story now goes on, however, in a world that is round, complete, and contained within itself. It no longer has any serious frontiers, no *terrae ignotae*, no enclosures and no beyond. Gertrude Stein thought that this is what really bothers people—the world being all here now and at that a small world, as they say. It is the refusal to live around on a round world that leads to localisms, isolationisms, organizations, central committees, hierarchies, and so on as well as the passion, on whatever pretext, for polar explorations and the stratosphere. And still, "Once upon a time the world was round and you could go on it around and around." It is really a world for children and for saints and for the human mind insofar as they exist and move without getting anywhere, as it is all there to them wherever they are, and whenever. And life on such a world would be continuous legend, as legend is wherever and whenever, not needing to wait or hurry or wish or be like anything else. And art would be simply saying what is there, not explaining it or denouncing it or advertising it but expressing it just as it is or playing games with it.

A French geography for children begins: "La terre est ron de comme une boule. La terre tourne sur elle-même. La terre ne repose sur rien." The work of Gertrude Stein is such a world—round like a ball, turning upon itself and resting on nothing. It offers the pleasures and the difficulties of such a world.

If the world is round and the gates are gone—if even the last open doors and iron curtains do go—the novel, at least according to the working definition in this chapter, is no longer possible except as a description of the collapse or desperate re-enforcement of enclosures. Perhaps it can go on very well as long as it knows what it is doing, that is,

171

describing an anachronistic reality and a dying set of values. But Proust has already covered that ground. Gertrude Stein only begins to extricate narrative from the novel, but it was a very vigorous beginning and based on a complete reality. *Brewsie and Willie, Ida,* and even *Lucy Church Amiably* belong to a new and round and open world.

6. *Meditations*

Someone once told Gertrude Stein that like George Washington she was impulsive and slow minded, and it is true because she never rushed her ideas through to a conclusion or a solution but preferred to live with them and play with them. For this reason she never articulated a system of ideas but she did write a great many meditations or essays. This kind of thing can take the form of a short prose piece as with Montaigne, or it can be quasi-theatrical as with Plato and Diderot, or it can take a poetical form, as with Pope's *Essay on Man* or Shelley's *Epipsychidion* or Tennyson's *In Memoriam* and so on. Now that ideas are mostly felt as ideology, as political weapons, one can scarcely separate them from a polemical atmosphere, and whenever they are uttered they have the quality of expecting contradiction or of laying down the law. Ideas are points, made or put across, and so must be conclusions or solutions. They rarely provoke a delight that is free from malice, they are not loved, and they are not amusing. But Shelley could still deal in ideas with the same poetical intensity as he sustained on skylarks and stars. And Diderot said "Les pensées ce sont mes catins." The erotic charm or sweetness or beauty of ideas may depend on the Hellenic spirit or the Latin, and it may very well be that it was the German philosophy of the last century that succeeded in making them imperative and necessary and no more. Whatever

173

happened it is too bad. One wishes ideas were not depressing, but they are.

They did not, however, depress Gertrude Stein, she was passionately fond of them. I once made the standard objection to a picture by Picabia, that it was too conceptual, and she answered that if it were not conceptual she would have nothing to do with it. But she was the opposite of academic, she felt that ideas should be constantly created or re-created out of experience, that they belong to the present and not to memory or authority. For her they came, as abstractions, as an intrinsic part of present experience, as a quality of it, and not as strayed into the present from the body of philosophical tradition.

Her quarrel with her brother Leo was more than a personal quarrel. It was his mission in life to make art into ideas and it was hers to make art of experience involving ideas. He could attempt an aesthetic system and have a cultivated taste, and he did, but she had to discover a new system with almost every book she wrote, and she had less a taste than a ravenous appetite for fullness and completeness of quality in whatever it was.

Her work did have a sort of logical progression, as I have roughly described it in the preceding chapters—from the isolation of present interior time to the collaboration with spatial existences, and then to the coordination of interior movement with movement in space, then to absolute movement or vibration, and finally to absolute eventfulness or narrative superseding the inside-outside situation—but her passage from one stage to another was governed less by knowing the next logical step than by impulse and the instinct for renovation or dépouillement, and it was often enough a lucky accident like being in Granada or Bilignin or America that helped to set her going. She said she had a great deal of inertia, and besides that she normally was having too good a time where she was to be

174

anxious about the next stage. "Come one come all," she says in *How to Write*, "this rock shall fly from its firm base as soon as I."[1] As a Stein she was enough of a stone never to leave her firm base in the present, but aside from that she did move and change, and often abruptly. As Picasso, while eternally Picasso, kept changing. "Plus ça change, plus c'est la même chose," and while recognizing that her ideas are usually intrinsic to the changes and stages there are some that are so very close to her essential quality and impulse one may say they never changed, and one may take them as an implicit ground or frame for her meditations as well as for her other work.

She was born with an enormous amount of what William James called the will to live. This is a fairly rare thing and is different from the will to be safe or right or superior or happy or what not. But the full realization of being alive requires the creation of or the absorption in things that are complete and final, or that are at least lived as if they were complete and final. This is why her writing is closer to religion and mathematics than to morals and science and history; these last are always full of loose ends and further connections and can rarely be made to be complete even in bits. This is why we have the terrific qualitative saturation of *Three Lives*, the continuous present and the universal paradigms of *The Making of Americans*, the isolations and disconnections of *Tender Buttons*, and the perpetual effort in the later works to make a thing contained within itself. This is why she could have nothing to do with the continuous incompleteness of consecutive action and dramatic stories and had to forego narrative until she had developed a sense—past rhythm, past movement, past vibration—of sheer happening as an absolute. She made the very useful distinction between being lively and being alive, as liveliness can be produced by incom-

1. *How to Write*, p. 312.

pletions, transiencies, suggestions and relativities, and while these with their kind of liveliness may be very pleasant and charming they are not thoroughly exciting as something really alive can be. This corresponds fairly closely to her distinction between saints and hysterics,[2] which allows hysterics their sensitivity and charm and brilliance but denies them the "individual force" of the saint, which is mainly felt in the totality of living presence, in the saint being all there at once. The saint may or may not be lively but he is completely alive.

One of her frequent bothers with her own work was, she said, that it often seemed to go dead just after it was written, though it had been hugely exciting and absorbing in the writing. Then on rereading she would lose herself in it—that is, let the work have its way and its own life— and it would come alive for her again. She rarely yielded to the temptation to write a conventionally lively or decorative work full of point-blank excitement and intoxication over anything, her work had to be alive and sober and exciting or nothing, even at the risk of seeming dead to everybody including herself. The unmitigated simplicity of vocabulary and expression in her later works can be readily understood as part of that instinct, but even the more difficult and strange works of the "middle period" are no doubt as simple as they could be, for what she was expressing. She did not even fully trust the liveliness that comes from excess of life, and she suspected inspiration of being a kind of drunkenness. Her form of excitement or exaltation was concentration and fullness of realization. This corresponded to, if it was not caused by, her physique, which was small and compact—"heavy set and seductive" as she said Henry James was.[3] A taller and more loosely

2. *The Autobiography of Alice B. Toklas,* p. 188.
3. *Four in America,* p. 155.

built person, if he really lives his writing, will naturally write another kind of thing.

To live her reality compactly and completely she had to reduce memory to little more than her language as she was writing, since memory splits or diffuses the attention fixed on the present object and makes the living with or in the object incomplete. At times even remembering what the object was and what it was for or about seemed to her a distraction from the realization of its immediate qualities and character. One may say that the isolation and extrication of immediate quality from the whole unending complex of practical relations and associated substantives has been the essential meaning of art in the first half of the 20th century. Earlier art has reorganized the whole complex upon immediate quality by a sort of harmonics, but the 19th century completely drowned immediate quality in the overelaboration of harmonics and the supersaturation with subject matter—take Browning or Brahms or Bouguereau—so that a gradual stylization and then a disconnection of quality from subject matter had to take place. Gertrude Stein said that this had to be done, the 20th century thing had to be created by Spain, which had no organization, and by America, which had an excess of it, that is, by Picasso and herself. What made his painting and her writing disturbing is that people had usually had the habit of first recognizing the subject matter—that is of settling their appetitive or muscular disposition toward it as they would toward its counterpart in a real situation—and then indulging in the intuition of quality. The settling of muscular disposition gave them the feeling of understanding and the erroneous impression that the intuition of quality was a part of the understanding or the same thing, whereas the understanding was really a way of getting rid of everything that was not the intuition of

177

quality or a way of moving the mind up to that intuition, or holding it there. Gertrude Stein and Picasso reduced these preliminaries of understanding to a minimum and produced sheer quality as directly and nakedly as possible. They both lived in it—at their best completely. Gertrude Stein is more difficult than Picasso because one can more readily take what goes on in paint qualitatively than one can what goes on in words, words being more habitually involved than lines and colors are in conveying information about the situations of real action—semantically. One does not understand a Picasso after recognizing the stray nose or table top, the rest is the simple experience of quality so intense and dramatic in itself that it holds the attention and excites and satisfies without the confusion of understanding. But when Gertrude Stein uses words and even numbers qualitatively, as experiential finalities and things in themselves, our attention is likely to fail because what normally keeps it up in words is information.

It is possible to accuse this isolation of quality, this thing existing in itself, of heresy in religion, of escapism in politics, of solipsism in philosophy, and of narcism if not worse in psychology. But it belongs to the everlasting and central impulse of art and life, only redoubling the insistence that the quality of experience in the here and now be everything and final.

Gertrude Stein did not argue herself into this position, she got there by the impulse of her whole nature and only later began to try to explain it to herself and others. Her first effort to explain the meaning of her work came as late as 1923, in *An Elucidation*. It is not really an explanation at all because a quality, a thing existing in itself, is not really explicable into terms of practicalities and reasons and principles. It is no explanation of red to say it is part of the spectrum or that it is there to stop automobiles. The only way to elucidate the color red as experienced is to compose in it or to give examples of it, and *An Elucidation* is mainly a series of examples of Stein prose.

She did later, in *Composition as Explanation,* in *Lectures in America,* in *Narration,* and passages in other books, settle down to explaining in connection with reasons and principles what she was about, but the pursuit of such connections is never ending and never complete and really substitutes the connections for the original thing itself. When ideas themselves are the subject matter, ordinary explanation or philosophical discourse stays with an idea only long enough to be sure it will stay put until we get on to the next one and so on, and while we may go back to the first now and then to check and make sure it is still there, that is the end of it. This process can very well disengage a quality of speed and brilliance and elegance, but it is rather limited. Gertrude Stein gets a greater range of quality out of ideas by staying with them, playing with them, turning them upside down and inside out, setting them against scenery and pigeons, against numbers and weather, against people and flowers, making them into little plays and poems and cadenzas, going for walks with them. Her meditations—among which I would include *An Elucidation, How to Write, An Acquaintance with Description, The Geographical History of America,* "Stanzas in Meditation," and certainly *Four in America*—are an activity which gives to ideas more than their rather tedious function of being true or being serviceable. They take on the quality of living and of being lived with. Ideas seem to have knocked off work and come to play croquet and tag and ring-around-a-rosy with Gertrude Stein, and often enough more strenuous games. They have probably not had so brilliant and active a leisure in English since Laurence Sterne. All work and no play makes Jack a dull boy, and it is also true of ideas. They are depressing now and stiff in the joints because during most of the 19th century they

179

did little but work. At least in English and German. In France and the Latin countries they kept a certain agility because of conversation and probably the athletic tradition of Catholic scholasticism. Currently we may hope that the demand for less work will lead to a positive sense of leisure which will extend to ideas. Ideas will always work, at least part time, but they should, even in the interest of their work, be given a chance to enjoy themselves. Gertrude Stein gave them a chance, on her time. She had undoubtedly learned something of how to do it from William James, who was extremely good at it, and even from the psychological laboratory under Münsterberg, but having gone on from Harvard to Paris she could do it more completely.

In her lectures the ideas are back at work and very much refreshed, but inevitably the games of the meditations are more exciting. It is a pity to interrupt them, but criticism is an interruption to start with, and I should like to call a few ideas out of their games for the chore of a short interview, choosing some that star or at least figure in most of her games.

Q: "How do you do."

A: "Very well I thank you."

Q: Would you care to make a statement?

A: Gladly. "If we say, Do not share, he will not bestow they can meditate, I am going to do so, we have organised an irregular commonplace and we have made excess return to rambling." [4]

Q: You will not mind if I ask what an irregular commonplace is?

A: Not at all, since the answer is anything. That is, anything is the answer. Or anything is an answer. But to come back to the question. Anything is at once typical and unique. And so anything is what "everybody knows and nobody knows," an irregular commonplace, and Miss Stein

4. *Portraits and Prayers,* p. 247.

was always writing the portrait of that, and of anything.

Q. Do go on.

A: I always do. It is just as well to ramble on about it after all. Anything, as I was saying, that comes before the normal mind in the normal life can be identified by name, and that aspect of it which has to do with our habitual practical purposes is obviously and clearly seen. But that same anything contains or involves a great many other aspects and qualities that everybody knows are there, even though everybody keeps his mind pretty well fixed on the single practical aspect and is only vaguely aware of the others, and strictly speaking does not know them.

Q: Can you give an illustration?

A: Everything is an illustration, but take any piece of land. Let alone the farmer and the real estate agent or the picnicker, one painter will see it flat, another painter will see it in depth, another as structure, another as fluffy, another as dark and light, another as spots and lines, another as still, another as changeable, another as full of its detail, another as a general expression or mood, and so on. But it is all the time the same commonplace piece of land. Likewise people and ideas are normally just as commonplace, but they are irregular since they do contain what is from the practical point of view an excess of aspects and qualities. If it were not for this excess nobody probably would go on living, because in it is all possibility and all novelty and all freedom. I think it was Voltaire who made that irregular commonplace, that paradox, that the superfluous is a very necessary thing. Which would remind me of the natural necessity of paradox, but it would be an excess to venture into it just now.

Q: Thank you very much. But why make excess return to rambling, as you say? Where has it been and what has it been doing?

A: It has been mainly in suggestion, exclaiming. As in,

181

what a woman! What a piece of land! Ah, Paree! But there has been a more sustained and exhaustively organized way of giving simultaneously a fairly large number of aspects, giving the commonplace a particular iridescence and a sonority, a harmonics, and that was the method of symbolism and of the 19th century impressionists, of Proust and Joyce and Pound and T. S. Eliot.

Q: And Dante. And Virgil. And Milton. And so on. Can you really complain of them?

A: No, not unless for a change you like a hard focus, and simplicity, and seeing things all in one plane or singly. Even then one does not so much complain as get interested in something else. Impressionism is fine but after you have had a lot of it you suddenly want something like cubism.

Q: And after cubism something like impressionism.

A: Or like Francis Rose or Eugene MacCown or the neoromantics. No doubt at all. Not after fifty years or so of something like cubism. That pendulum has been swinging and swinging since the caves of Altamira. Shall we return from rambling now and keep to the subject?

Q: Yes, though I am beginning to think any subject naturally rambles around by itself and to keep to it one has to ramble around after it. But we can return to the text. How does "Do not share, he will not bestow they can meditate, I am going to do so" organize an irregular commonplace? I appreciate that we had returned to rambling and excess, but what kind of organization is that?

A: Well, suppose you have a commonplace group of people before you and you wish to describe them, as a painter would wish to describe a piece of land in front of him. The painter can select out of it and isolate certain shapes or accents on which to arrange a composition in shapes or accents, rather than a composition in depths or effects of light and texture or as a setting for figures, and so on. Just so, out of your group of people you can select

182

certain active attitudes to make a composition of them, rather than record the differences in the color of their eyes and hair, or in their political views, or tell a story involving all of them. You can say, Do not share, he will not bestow they can meditate, I am going to do so. Or you can apply the method to the universal and variable drama of grocers, and say:

First grocer. I am sincere.
Second grocer. I believe in service.
Third grocer. I love my mother.
Fourth grocer. I am rich.[5]

Or you can color the drama by giving the characters pleasant names and broaden it by making the objects of their attitudes anything at all, that is, "it," and say:

Harry. Should it be known.
Ashley. Could it have come
Amelia. Would it be known
Nuña. Or would it have come[6]

And there you are.

Q: Where? Let us ramble back to the first example. It could have been done in the way you say, and I see that we have a set of statements abstracted from a reality, but all I see in it is a loose set of abstractions. Oh I do see that the postures, the dispositions and relations of the characters of four people in one moment have been "tenuously" conceived, and registered in an irreducible outline, as if Picabia were drawing. That much I can see and I think I like it. But I don't recognize, in that much, an organization.

A: But any sentence is in itself an organization of ex-

5. *Operas and Plays*, p. 126.
6. *Last Operas and Plays*, p. 191.

perience, and in that little passage there is also the pictorial organization of simple juxtaposition, the verbal situation changes from the imperative to the third person singular to the third person plural to the first person singular. We have rhythm and rhyme, we have a style that is compact, simple, decisive. It is all, both in the manner and the literal sense, full of a vital tension. This tension is stabilized by the fact that Do not share, he will not bestow, they can meditate, I am going to do so, all, as sentences, express a relation between the present and the future, a relation that is modulated from sentence to sentence through several degrees of immediacy and closes in its highest degree of immediacy, its major or tonal center, so to say: *I am going to do so.* It is, to be bright about it, a tension of tenses. Also, the vocabulary is harmonized to the tenses: the laxer "bestow" and "meditate" to the negative and potential futures, the sharper and monosyllabic "share" and "do so" to the more present futures. All the aspects of the passage are informed with a single intention, or, if you like, sustain a continuing vibration. As a verbal plastic one might almost say it is overorganized.

Q: Yes, but it is not very organized toward telling me anything about the group of people. As a vehicular organization I question it.

A: How much do you want conveyed? Actually the passage conveys enough, like an outline drawing or silhouette or X ray or snapshot. Yet from the point of view of its intrinsic organization, its internal coherence and entity, the very small percentage of information it carries is mere courtesy, like the eggs and apples in arithmetic or the rubber balls in topology.

Q: Then it is not really about people, that is, some four actual people once?

A: Not quite. Four people once did, by being together, bring into being, for Gertrude Stein, that thing.

184

Q: So, as a matter of fact, it is about people?

A: It was once, in a way. But it is now complete in itself. Its "about" relationship, which was never essential, is now cut off or atrophied. Even the original relationship of these abstractions and the quality of their organization to the actual people was more a matter of "here" and "out of" than "about." If it were "about" anything still and essentially, if its meaning depended on that relationship, it would not be complete. The completeness of "two plus two equals four" does not now depend on being about apples or dinosaurs or whatever originally led to it as an observation.

Q: But "two plus two" can be applied in many cases of quantity, even if its completeness is in itself.

A: Of course. Literature is not quite arithmetic but it comes close to it in proverbs and some poetry, particularly quotable poetry. One counts apples by referring them to numbers, and one can count the quality of a situation or what not by referring it to proverbs or a quotation or for that matter a word. But these have a reality of their own which does not depend on their occasional use of being referred to or on the experience that first occasioned them. Nursery rhymes, advertising slogans, the declensions and conjugations in grammar books, all have to some degree this disconnected reality. The four sentences quoted cannot be universally applied, but often enough to make them a commonplace a group of people will demonstrate them. A group will present variously the peremptory, the reserved, the competent, and the determined together, and just barely outside the central focus of what they consider they are there for. The four sentences moreover reproduce exactly the tension and animation produced by several different personal intentions together. It is what everybody knows, since the way one sits, the tone of one's voice, all of one's behavior in such a group is qualified by one's ap-

185

prehension of it. But nobody knows it articulately or in isolation because it has not been put directly into words that are more than a historical account of a particular occasion or a contribution to the academic study of group dynamics. This little passage does put it in durable words.

Q: Does it really imply all that? Is art that long? I mean, am I, in reading some four short sentences, to read all that and more into them?

A: No, not unless you care to. All that or something like it goes into making the sentences solid and complete and possessed of themselves, into sustaining their quality to the utmost. Just as a great deal of climatology and aeronautics goes into the simplest flight. But that is nothing, or need be nothing, to you as a passenger.

Q: If you wish to call the passage a flight, I follow the parallel, but how can I personally tell, while reading the passage, while in it, that we are off the ground?

A: You will know you are up by the look of things— they will be very familiar and all there but very strange and simpler. Like proverbs or declensions or titles. You can also tell by the intensity of movement combined with not seeming to be getting anywhere.

Q: But actually by this time I am tired of airplanes, real or metaphorical. If left to myself I think I prefer to walk.

A: To ramble? If so you will be moving without getting anywhere except where you are from moment to moment. But you may be intensely there, and in that case you are making a Stein composition of your time. You are in a state of perpetual discovery and quite within the commonplace. It is all clear and you are not lost. And nothing is worse in such a situation than to have somebody telling you step by step where you are on the map. It vitiates your being where you are. And in rambling around in a Stein composition one can very well feel that explanation and

186

criticism are a gross intrusion, especially since Gertrude Stein herself eminently left you alone with her work. Even after she had indulged in explanation she asked, "Do you know because I tell you so, or do you know, do you know." [7]

Q: And the answer?

A: After the question there is a stage direction: "(Silence)." Which in its way is a hopeful answer, at least a prayer, because if you are really busy knowing and not learning you do not answer questions.

* * *

A: "He he he he and he and he and and he and he and he and and as and as he and as he and he." [8]

Q: You have the giggles.

A: Not I, but Picasso. That is part of a portrait of Picasso. That is what is, we gather from other sources, his "high whinnying Spanish giggle."

Q: I would not know unless you told me so.

A: But you could know perfectly well a sequence of fairly perpetual assertions of a single masculine subject and that whatever is being done by Picasso he is doing it simply and nakedly as or qua a very singular very masculine very active subject. That his Spanish giggle sounds like the English word for the essence of the man and his work is just one of the miracles that came to Gertrude Stein with an unbelievable frequency. They should be gathered, against the day of her proper canonization.

* * *

A: *I think I won't*
I think I will
I think I will
I think I won't

7. *Last Operas and Plays*, p. 88.
8. *Portraits and Prayers*, p. 23.

I think I won't
I think I will
I think I will
I think I won't
I think I won't
I think I will
I think I will
I think I won't
I think I will
I think I won't
I think I will
I think I won't
I think I will
I think I won't
I think I won't
I think I won't
I think I won't
I think I will
I think I won't
Of course
I think I will
I think I won't
I think I won't
I think I will
This is a good example if you do not abuse it.[9]

Q: An example?

A: Of Gertrude Stein, but of art that is alive. It is implicitly—as here explicitly—an all but continuous insistence on deciding, on choosing and refusing.

Q: It gives me a feeling that she has just left her motor running.

A: So she has, so that you can listen to it without distraction.

9. *Portraits and Prayers,* pp. 255–256.

Q: Am I actually to confuse the art of literature with internal combustion engines?

A: It seems one has to confuse literature with something if one is to think about it articulately. One can very well measure the authenticity and power of a work by its truth to its time. There are other measures, but the truth to its time is most easily seen by comparing or confusing it with the typical real created product of the time, in our case the internal combustion engine surely. There is nothing terribly wrong with letting the natural power of a natural subject pull the created thing along except that it constitutes a horse-and-buggy situation and puts you in a horse-and-buggy time. You become schizochronic, if you please, and sentimental. "We have all forgotten the horse" should be true, but there is a minority chic and a majority relaxation in going in for horses and horse-drawn literature.

Q: But why should we forget the horse?

A: Because it cannot be completely exciting any more. You are not really living your life when you amuse yourself with horses. And art should be an intense and real way of living one's life, actually and not retrospectively.

Q: But what was that "of course" late in the passage?

A: The motor missed.

Q: I think it missed the horse.

A: Yes, it is human. When it abandons its own energy of choice and says "of course" to anything, either it is coasting or it is letting a natural thing do the moving. But I confess it is a pleasure and refreshing to have it happen, at least in the proportion in which the passage has it happen. It saves us from making a mechanical necessity of choice.

Q: Let us not abuse the example.

* * *

189

A: *An example of an event.*
If it is an event just by itself is there a question.
Tulips is there a question.
Pets is there a question.
Furs is there a question.
Folds is there a question.
Is there anything in question.[10]

Q: Internal-combustion or horse-drawn, where is this getting us?

A: Here.

Q: I beg your pardon?

A: ". . . all words furnish here."

Q: If you insist.

A: Only if one insists. Here is not so easily reached.

* * *

A: "I think the reason I am important is that I know everything." [11]

Q: I may giggle?

A: Of course. But after your natural moment, and mine, and hers, it is worth saying that the remark is true too. She did not know everything in the sense of erudition, although her erudition was vast. She knew everything in the sense that she was almost constantly "here," she did directly know everything that came before her, instead of remembering its history or its purposes or its connections. She let it be "here." It amounts to a special discipline, this special concentration and act of presence, and her mastery of it was a genuine importance. Most of us develop another sort of efficiency, which suppresses everything that is not purpose and connection, or we develop an erudition which drowns the object in its history, purposes, connections. We rarely know an object directly with its immediate

10. *Portraits and Prayers*, p. 258.
11. *How to Write*, p. 169.

190

qualities, which are most actually and really it. In this way Gertrude Stein did know everything. She even contrived to know a good deal of what she remembered.

*   *   *

A: "Lilacs lilies vases Voltaire and Basket. It would be easy to imagine a conversation." [12]

Q: Surely not too easy?

A: She didn't write the conversation.

Q: Why not?

A: I wonder. She could have done it. She could perfectly write it in the character of lilies, in the character of vases, in the character of lilacs, in the character of Voltaire, and most certainly in the character of her dog Basket. Her knowledge of the immediate qualities of lilies and the rest was vivid enough to allow her to imagine what they would say about anything and how they would say it. Suppose all the characters got together to explain to Basket the meaning of roundabout or of Thursday. It would be, if not easy, at least not impossibly difficult, and it would have been enchanting.

Q: Fragrant, at least.

A: And delicate. The trouble would be in having it all constantly depend on its likenesses to lilies, lilacs, vases, Voltaire, and Basket, so that the writer and the reader would have to be forever remembering and recognizing lilacs and Voltaire and so on in every little bit. But to use the character as a "tuning fork" or a key signature for any subject at all would be more exciting if less delectable. Once started in a key and time one does not remember B-flat or six-eighths, one just goes on with it and keeps creating it, but as the locale of more exciting events.

*   *   *

12. *How to Write,* p. 346.

A: "I have never at any time expressed a part." [13]

Q: But she must have. Any whole composition is composed of parts, even a sentence is composed of parts.

A: Yes, but as to *expression,* not its articulation, one may, and Gertrude Stein did, write as if every instant of writing were complete in itself, as if in the act of writing something were continuously coming true and completing itself, not as if it were leading to something, or only coming there to go to make up something else, or to pave the way for something else not yet arrived. This is one of the reasons for her wild numbering of chapters, pages, volumes, etc., and for the prodigious stage direction in *Four Saints:* "Repeat first act."

Q: So we get something like a random list or a dictionary that has renounced the alphabet, or an inventory? Something like a charm bracelet or a necklace of odd stones or the visual composition in a painter like Bosch? Is it composition?

A: Well yes, even if that were all. The mere tenuity of connection could be a sufficiently exciting thing in itself, especially in a time of disaggregation. But while the materials of a Stein composition are often practically and historically disparate, there is a sustaining continuity, not only by the saturation of stylistic quality generally but of intensity. Intensity is really the last question, however it is reached. The familiar methods of causal structure, of analytical or reportorial exhaustion, of the vehement moral message, of lyrical emotion, and so on, succeed with anybody only insofar as they produce an intensely existing and absorbing thing. The props and external articulations of the intensity can be almost anything, but with Gertrude Stein they are mainly movements and relations and qualities, both named and reproduced. Let me spare us a list of the devices, such as repetition, alternation, isolation, compres-

13. *Geographical History,* p. 149.

192

sion, collision, departure, etc., which generate, out of discontinuous materials and forms—materials and forms which have "parts" and are "composed"—a continuum of intensity, which is not a sum of parts. She was "expressing" a continuum of present movement, making it intrinsic to the work itself, and this inner thing is complete, not as a construction but as a continuum.

Q: I am uneasy again. It was a strain thinking in terms of internal combustion and now we are getting into something like magnetic fields and we are not far from higher mathematics and metaphysics. Are we still talking about literature? Even if we had the knowledge to talk professionally about mathematics and metaphysics would we be talking about literature?

A: No, or only indirectly. But the realities we are talking about have been made clear and articulate in other than literary terms, and we lack a specific terminology for the literary forms of those realities. Sooner or later criticism will have to get used to thinking in terms of forces, tensions, movements, speeds, attractions, etc., as well as in terms of constructs and animals—not because science says so or philosophy says so at all but because life is conducted more and more in those terms and it is the way life is conducted in a time that is the prime source of steady energy and solid reality in a work that outlasts its time. This kind of composition is getting to be more and more the composition of reality as everyone sees it. It amused Gertrude Stein to find that her early arrangements and abstractions, which had seemed to be highly acrobatic and gratuitous if refined formal exercises, were turning out to be literal transcriptions of the most evident realities, that is the same abstractions and arrangements on which life is more and more consciously conducted by people at large.[14] It is true that we are more comfortable in the composition of

14. Cf. *Composition as Explanation*, p. 9.

19th century life and literature, in which an actual or a mentioned cup of tea was part of an hour which was part of a day which was part of a week, month, season, or year, which was part of say the annals of Britain, which were part of the general onward evolution of something that was part of a cosmic order. A sentence was part of a paragraph which was part of a chapter which was part of a book which was part of a shelf of books which was part of England or America or France and so on. Something belonged to everything automatically. But nothing now is really convincingly a part of anything else; anything stands by itself if at all and its connections are chance encounters.

Q: If it is true, it sounds scary. Do you mean to make it sound exhilarating?

A: Officially of course it is scary. But it is a godsend to an artist. It leaves everything open, and so many realities can still be made. Not dreamed, if you please, but made.

*   *   *

A: "Letting it be not what it is like." [15]

Q: Letting anything be?

A: Again, anything.

Q: So anything becomes, a least as a whole, unique and new. Suppose I let the work of Gertrude Stein too be just itself and not compare it with anything, not even its time or ours, not the reality out of which it came. Suppose I do not recognize anything in it particularly, but come to it with the simple completely occupied intuition I might apply to an unfamiliar dancer or landscape or circus. I agree that the material is intellectual, as it is words with their meanings foremost, and syntax and grammar, which are intellectual arrangements, but if the words and their relations and movements are taken qualitatively, simply presented to the intuition, is this not after all converting

15. *An Acquaintance with Description*, p. 6.

194

intellectual things into the unintellectual, into brute experience again? Is it not precisely a barbarism, the reduction of intellect to sensation or emotion? Gertrude Stein was accused often enough of barbarism and infantilism in her writing, and, even if the bulk of the accusation does not stick, is there not at least this much in it? If we let everything be not what it is like, renouncing comparison and identification, which are surely the foundation of intellection, are we not left with our mere senses and emotions, however we sophisticate their objects with logical contrivance? Even if the sensations produced are subtle, rare, and exciting, strong without being gross, and so on, are we not reverting to the refined type of barbarism known as decadence?

A: I think not. In the first place intellect is busier than usual in reading a work by Gertrude Stein, in distinguishing likenesses and differences, changes and repetitions in a very great range of matters and forms; the restriction is simply that this goes on inside the work itself—intensely inside it—and not back and forth between the work and other things at large. But this restriction of the intellectual activity is a concentration of it. That was one question, and I think we may at last forget it. The other question was very large, but I may have an answer. Is it barbarism of a kind if the net result of the intellectual activity is not logically articulate knowledge but felt experience? Is that the question?

Q: It sounds a little harmless the way you have put it, as if it were about all art, and not about an extreme kind of it. In most art the intellectual element, the ideas, even when their expression is an experience, do open the experience upon the perspectives of knowledge whose presence could be called civilization. Such art could be called a vivification of that presence by actualizing it into experience. An art which is opaque to those perspectives, in which

195

the ideas are completely enclosed within the experience, could perhaps reasonably be called barbarous.

A: Let me come at this from the side. If you take the will to live as your point of departure and your basic force, and living fully as your end in view, intellect is to be taken as a means for realizing that fullness, somehow or other, with or without civilization and what you call its perspectives of knowledge. The realization itself is a sensation, an absorption in quality. We are told that the forms of our thought as well as our art are merely symbols, that all our activity is merely ritual and has no reality outside of the mere event and the experience of man. If that is so, if only experience can be real, any real thing is primarily qualitative, and gets its reality by being vividly present to the intuition, not by being connected with something else except as such connections provide an intuition of steadiness and location and equilibrium and so completeness. Indeed all the constructions of intellect intend so to arrange experience that it will provide a constant sensation of completeness and fullness, not unlike the ostrich egg Gertrude Stein kept on her desk. Like innocent ostrich eggs, intellectual schemes are usually preoccupied with coherence, balance, unity, continuity, and so on, but usually create them by elaborating the connections between reasonably large numbers of things until they stick together into a single conglomeration. The effort of a good deal of art in the 20th century has been so to intensify the movement or the quality of a single thing or a very few things together that it will make a complete thing to the intuition and self-sustaining. Its reality depends on the intensity of its quality, not on its connections and correspondences and distances from other things in a perspective. As with an ostrich egg.

Q: Exactly, and is not the energy which creates in the work enough intensity to give it a reality in isolation mere narrow animal enthusiasm, and is not the absorption of the

196

whole attention in such a thing a simple barbaric infatuation with violence of quality? As with a fancy for ostrich eggs.

A: As living energy it is no doubt animal, but since the human mind is there the energy is kept from running off into action, its natural course, and is so concentrated as to move while staying where it is—like the water of a fountain. One may say that barbarism and decadence alike consist in the failure of the mind to concentrate vital energy on the present—that the barbarian and the decadent prefer to be carried through it or away from it, into action or reminiscent feeling, by a set of ideas or by violent and suggestive quality. This automatism of response away from or through or out of the object as against staying with it, this inattention so to speak, is barbaric and is decadent though it does have more respectable forms.

Q. The Faustian and so on?

A: And so on. But that would lead us out of this question. We can simply say what is no news, that human life exceeds its civilizations. Faust and Don Juan are outside of civilization, though the plays and operas about them are probably civilized enough and impose on them precisely the concentrated present that is civilization.

Q: But there is another version, that civilization consists in a deliberately cultivated tradition, in considering the present in the light of the past and of a plausible future. One may even say that civilization consists in the conduct of action according to ends remembered from the past and projected into the future, and in treating the present as mere transition or viability.

A: One may indeed, and embrace the prevalent notion that administration and education are the essence of it. If civilization administrates and educates it is only while it is relaxing; its real activity is creation and what it creates is present reality and the reality of the present. The barbarian,

197

the decadent, the administrator and the educator take reality for granted, they rarely do not suppose that reality already exists, to be exploited or perpetuated or lamented or escaped from. The new realities, created in its present by civilization, are, however, the result of direct collaboration with, or opposition to, the given or left-over world, the "reality" which is not vivid or complete or clear enough as it is, to be perfectly real to the mind. A reality which does not defer or refer to it at all can be eminently a civilized thing.

Q. Is civilization the question, though? Civilization is questionable, and currently very much in question, but is it really in art the final question?

A: I think not. If art is, really is, it is an absolute and consequently our question is not the service of art to civilization but of civilization to art. And is a civilized art better than a barbarian or decadent art?

Q: Why hesitate?

A: If I say yes I shall seem to decide against the Scythians and Verlaine, and what use would that be? But there is this, that civilization is more conscious of more realities and more qualities more continuously than the barbarian and the decadent, and if it succeeds in making its art as real as its world or more real, the art evidently is broader and richer and fuller and more intense, in a word more real, than barbarian or decadent art which is incidental to another reality. So that the work of Gertrude Stein at least means to be civilized and is preoccupied with a specifically civilized problem, the creation of reality. So that our talk about civilization has that much point.

Q: But surely history has some connection with civilization, surely perspective has something to do with it.

A: Not necessarily. Civilization in its health feels that anything *is* fully real only as it is fully present to the mind. History can very well be used for isolating a present thing and keeping it steady, which is a civilized use, but not when

198

history refers or pushes a present thing away. In more religious centuries the mind of God, full of numbered hairs and fallen sparrows, did serve to assure everyone that, appearances to the contrary, everything is completely real whether the attention of the single human mind is on it or not. In the 19th century the presumable intentions of history or destiny served the same purpose, and now science does it. But civilization has to make everything real, not elsewhere with memories and hopes but with and to the present human mind. It has to make experience complete, not to God, nor as it connects with a universal system of any kind, but to the mind of the human being. Civilization believes in the finite, in the here and now, and lives there, since the human mind cannot be anything but here and now. If it has to deal with infinity it uses concrete symbols and rituals. Elsewhere and past and future can be made more or less present to the mind by memory and foresight and suggestion but very rarely completely present. It is the same with stories and systems, the completeness of the present parts is vitiated by their being provisory to the completeness of the whole, which is not yet. It is the same with anything that is essentially related to anything outside itself. Gertrude Stein tried to make a complete and real thing of anything she loved, and that was almost anything. Her intensity of unreserved presentness brings it about that her words were written and have to be read as if they were sentences, her sentences as if they were sonnets or paragraphs, and her paragraphs as if they were epics. For example, this sentence, which is and is printed as a complete poem:

"He likes to be with her so he says does he like to be with her so he says." [16]

Do you see how the movement and tension and balance of that are really the same thing as in a sonnet or a canzone?

16. *Before the Flowers of Friendship Faded Friendship Faded* (Plain Edition, 1931), p. 24.

Q: Not quite. Mind you, if all that you say is not true it is at least a very likely story, and I have no doubt that it was all real and intellectual and present enough to Gertrude Stein as she wrote. But her work, like that sentence you just quoted and which I admit is very prettily turned, does not give me a vivid sense of reality, it does not get me completely into it as it seems to do you. It is too disembodied and has no relation to things as I have known them or expect them. I feel I am barely in contact with it. I am willing to be enough of a barbarian to like to feel I know what it means in terms of action and the context I live in.

A: Try taking the words as events in themselves. Or sit down and read. Forget this talk about her work and do not prepare to have an opinion of your own to tell. Simply read her work as if that were to be all. Though even a determined and civilized act of presence may not hold you there. What holds one to any writer, as she said,[17] is not clarity to the practical understanding but his force of meaning. Her own work undeniably contains an extraordinary force, an elemental force of being, that holds many readers whether they understand it or not, and often in spite of themselves. That is after all a normal situation created by female forces. To say nothing of any extraordinary reality. Some of her work may well be bad, and certainly some of her most devoted admirers can take a violent dislike to some of it, but it is all an expression of the same force, which is a big one dealing in the last human realities. She seriously created, in the midst of our world, which was falling away under habits and memories and mechanisms of words and ideas, a new reality. The elements of that reality were implicit in the life of the 20th century—the intense isolation of anyone and anything, the simple gratuity of existence, the fantastic inventiveness, and the all but total lack of memory—but it was Gertrude Stein who made that implicit reality most distinct and posi-

17. *Four in America*, pp. 127–128.

tive and completely real to the reading mind, as Picasso
made it clear to the eye.

Q: It has been said often that it is a classical reality. I
can see it may be Spanish or American, given the existence
of self-sustaining Spanish ritual and the American gadget-
in-itself, but why classical?

A: There are too many answers, but one is that as the
Greeks isolated quantity and space directly out of experience and made them articulate in numbers and geometry,
and then made everything else articulate in those terms—
the terms and products being independent of experience
and action though derived from them—just as Gertrude
Stein and Picasso have isolated quality and movement, and
made them articulate, she in words,[18] and he in line and
color.[19] They both stabilized their abstractions against the
most essential of the older classical abstractions, Gertrude
Stein using numbers qualitatively and Picasso using geometry qualitatively. They are again classical in their insistence on an absolute present free of progress and suggestion, and their use of the flat plane.[20] The flat plane in Gertrude Stein's work is the simple and isolated present, but
also the composition of words with their simple unassoci-
ated meanings, related to each other on the page and not
to particular complexes of meaning presumably behind
them. The trouble is that we still have the habit of reading
in depth though we have more or less learned to look at

18. The identification of words with money rests on the isolation of value, not quantity.

19. The "movement" in Picasso's paintings and drawings varies,
but it is mainly in the "eventfulness" of the lines and colors, often
in the implicit gestures of the forms and too often in the gesticu-
lation of the subject matter. The static and merely demarcating
function of the older classical draughtsmanship and color is frequent in Picassos, but as a stabilizing element.

20. Cf. *Geographical History*, p. 147: "The human mind has
neither identity nor time and when it sees anything has to look
flat."

things flat. Classical literatures are to be read flat, but we are educated in 19th century and romantic depth. We can get the baroque, which struggles between flat and deep, and we can get Proust and Seurat for the same reason, but the really successfully completely flat classical plane is difficult for us, in reading at least. Not, however, in the way we live. We really do not, unless somebody tells us to, bother our heads with our roots and profundity. In the matter of roots we are not oaks but tumbling weeds, exposed to the caprice of the weather and the grace of God.

Q: And if we do not like the way we live? One may find the 20th century not at all endearing.

A: Anyone may like it or not, naturally. Picasso on the whole does not. Gertrude Stein happened to like it. Indeed she was in love with it. She knew as well as anyone what was wrong with the world but she could not help knowing it was also beautiful and loving it for that. Her everlasting gaiety came from that as much as from an incurable American optimism.

But our favorite question—Where does it come from?—is not really in order. It is an evasion of ostrich eggs to inquire about ostriches: Gertrude Stein was thoroughly Gertrude Stein, not what she was from or like. She, like anything that persistently is, does not really abide our explanations and comparisons. But having fatally a human liking for a resemblance we may like to remember, she could look like a Roman emperor or like a Buddha or like Picasso's portrait of her.

Though very likely her truest expression was the beautiful and blessedly inappropriate smile of Greek archaic statues. They look into a world that is strange but not alien, not dark and mysterious but full of self-evident and pleasurable wonders. So did she, and her work describes it. And more, her work is such a world.

202

Just before she died she asked, "What *is* the answer?" No answer came. She laughed and said, "In that case, what is the question?" Then she died.

Those were her last words, but they say what she had always been saying.

Appendix

The following lists are a rough guide to the stylistic periods and occupations of Gertrude Stein. The works listed are chosen from works published to date and are either major works, in the sense of being well known, or clear examples of a style.

In compiling these lists I have used as a guide the bibliography by Robert Bartlett Haas and Donald Clifford Gallup, entitled *A Catalogue of the Published and Unpublished Writings of Gertrude Stein* (Yale University Library, 1941).

Naturalism and the Continuous Present, 1902–1911

> *Things as They Are*
> *Three Lives*
> *The Making of Americans*
> "Miss Furr and Miss Skeene"
> "Many Many Women"
> "Matisse"
> "Picasso" (first portrait)
> "Playing"
> "Four Dishonest Ones"
> "Nadelman"
> "Galeries Lafayettes"

"Mi-careme" (1912)
"A Long Gay Book" (first half)

The Visible World as Simply Different, 1911–*ca*. 1921

Tender Buttons
"A Long Gay Book" (second half)
Portrait of Mabel Dodge at the Villa Curonia
"Susie Asado"
"Preciosilla"
"Guillaume Apollinaire"
"A Sweet Tail"
"In the Grass. On Spain"
"Americans"
"France"
"England"

The Visible World with Movement (First Plays), 1913–1922

"What Happened, a Play"
"Old and Old, a Play"
"Pink Melon Joy"
"Please Do Not Suffer, a Play"
"Mexico, a Play"
"Counting Her Dresses, a Play"
"An Exercise in Analysis, a Play"
Have They Attacked Mary. He Giggled. (A Political Caricature)
"Scenes from the Door"
"Reread Another, a Play"
"Objects Lie on a Table, a Play"
"A Circular Play"

The Play as Movement and Landscape, 1922–1932 [1]

"Lend a Hand or Four Religions"
"Am I To Go or I'll Say So. A Play in Places"
"Paisieu"
"Civilization. A Play"
"A Manoir"

The Melodic Drama, Melodrama, and Opera, 1922–1946

"Saints and Singing, a Play"
"Lend a Hand or Four Religions"
Four Saints in Three Acts
"A Lyrical Opera"
"Their Wills. A Bouquet. An Opera"
"Say It with Flowers, a Play at Tragedy
"The Five Georges, a Play"
"They Must. Be Wedded. To Their Wife. A Play"
"A Play a Lion for Max Jacob"
"A Play of Pounds"
"Short Sentences"
"Doctor Faustus Lights the Lights"
Yes Is for a Very Young Man
The Mother of Us All

1. In 1922 the "Spanish" period and the strictly "painting" end. Two discursive elements begin: melody and calligraphy. Although these had been present before, they do not disengage themselves until 1920. They dominate from 1922 to 1928. In 1928 the melody and calligraphy are further attenuated and intensified by being based mainly on syntax and the syntactical movement in phrases and sentences. This highly lyrical period lasts until 1932. But like almost all the "periods" it contains startling reversions to earlier methods, as "A Manoir" reverts to the landscape manner of *Lucy Church Amiably* and *Four Saints*. "A Manoir" was written in 1932, and I have extended the "landscape" period to include it, though that period properly ends in 1928. The division of Gertrude Stein's work into periods cannot be strict.

207

Calligraphy and Melody, 1920–1932

"A Valentine to Sherwood Anderson"
"An Instant Answer or One Hundred Prominent Men"
An Elucidation
A Book Concluding with As a Wife Has a Cow a Love Story
"Are There Six or Another Question"
"Wherein the South Differs from the North"
"And So. To Change So. A Fantasy on Three Careers"
"Fifteenth of November, T. S. Eliot"
"Jean Cocteau"
An Acquaintance with Description
"Three Sitting Here"
Lucy Church Amiably
Useful Knowledge

Syntax as Movement, Vibration, and Drawing, 1928–1940

How to Write
"George Hugnet"
Before the Flowers of Friendship Faded Friendship Faded
"The Five Georges"
Four in America
"Meditations in Stanzas" (or "Stanzas in Meditation")
The Geographical History of America
Ida
"How She Bowed to Her Brother"

History and Legend, 1930–1946

The Autobiography of Alice B. Toklas
"Daniel Webster, a Play"

"Madame Recamier, an Operatic Drama"
"At Present. Contemporaries. A Play"
Ida
Picasso
Paris France
"Doctor Faustus Lights the Lights"
The Mother of Us All
Brewsie and Willie
Four in America
The World Is Round

INDEX

212

214

217